THE EVERYDAY DAIRY-FREE COOKBOOK

THE
EVERYDAY
DAIRY-FREE
COOKBOOK

Over 180 Delicious Recipes to Make Eating a Pleasure

MILLER ROGERS AND EMILY WHITE

SURREY BOOKS · CHICAGO

The Everyday Dairy-Free Cookbook
is published by Surrey Books, Inc.,
230 E. Ohio St., Suite 120, Chicago, IL 60611.

First U. S. edition: 1 2 3 4 5
(First published by Grub Street, London, England.)

This book is manufactured in the United States of America.

Library of Congress Cataloging-in-Publication data
Rogers, Miller.
   The everyday dairy-free cookbook; recipes for lactose intolerants/
   Miller Rogers and Emily White.—1st U. S. ed.
      p. cm.
Includes index.
ISBN 1-57284-051-X (pbk.)
1. Milk-free diet—Recipes. I. White, Emily, 1967 - II. Title.
   RM234.5.R64 2003
   641.5'63—dc21   2002152311

Distributed to the trade by Publishers Group West.

Note: When making any of the recipes in this book, only
follow one set of measures at a time, i.e., metric or North
American (imperial).

Contents

FOREWORD

Between 30 and 50 million North Americans are lactose intolerant. A shocking figure—until you consider lactose intolerance for what it really is: a natural condition, a biological trait as unremarkable as olive skin or blue eyes.

Lactose, the sugar found in milk, is broken down by the enzyme lactase. In most of the world's population, lactase is produced only by infants, to aid in the digestion of mother's milk. The exception is people of northern European descent, whose diet for generations has been heavy in milk, cheese and cream—resulting in the production of lactase in adulthood. This group's influence is obvious in North American dietary culture: ice cream is a favorite dessert, children learn that milk builds strong bones and you can order almost anything with extra cheese.

Fortunately for the many people who come from different cultural traditions, times are changing. The demand for dairy-free cuisine will continue to grow with our diversifying population. For the 75% to 90% of North Americans with African, Asian or Native heritage who are lactose intolerant, relief is in sight as more grocery stores and restaurants address the growing market gap.

Ethical concerns over animal treatment and the impact of agricultural practices on the environment are causing more and more people to find alternatives to dairy products. National rates of obesity, coronary artery disease and diabetes are skyrocketing as well, and foods low in cholesterol and saturated animal fat are urgently needed.

Whether it's a matter of preference or necessity, *The Everyday Dairy-Free Cookbook* provides many simple and delicious solutions to dairy-free eating. From Mushroom and Walnut Strudel to Blueberry Muffins and Apple Pie, there is something for everyone who wants good-tasting, easy-to-prepare recipes free of milk and milk products.

As understanding of the condition increases, lactose intolerance becomes a far less distressing diagnosis. With *The Everyday Dairy-Free Cookbook*, lactose intolerance loses even its nuisance status. This recipe collection finally provides a satisfying answer to the dairy-free eater's enduring question "What foods can I enjoy?"

Suzanne Havala Hobbs, Dr. PH, MS, RD
Adjunct Assistant Professor
Department of Health Policy and Administration
School of Public Health
The University of North Carolina at Chapel Hill

INTRODUCTION

The word "allergy" is bandied around so often and appears to be the cause of so many health problems that it seems we have been overtaken by an epidemic of allergies. People claim to be allergic to almost anything, including sunlight, pollution, cell phones, most foods, the buildings they work in and even their boss or spouse!

By definition, an allergy is a hypersensitivity to a specific substance, such as insect stings, food, pollen, mold or dust. The substance causing the reaction is called an allergen. For most people insect stings, food, pollen, mold or dust are harmless. For the allergic person, reactions can range from mild symptoms, such as sneezing and itchy, red eyes in the case of pollen-induced hay fever, to life-threatening anaphylactic shock caused by eating peanuts or being stung by a bee.

While many North Americans have probably experienced the minor discomfort of seasonal hay fever, far fewer have ever experienced a true food allergy. In the United States, only 2 to 2 1/2 percent of the population suffers from food allergies, about 6 to 7 million Americans, according to the Food Allergy & Anaphylaxis Network, a nonprofit organization dedicated to increasing awareness about food allergies. Of the Americans with food allergies, nearly 3 million suffer from peanut or tree nut allergies. In Canada, 0.3% to 7.5% of children and 1% to 3% of adults are affected by food allergies, according to the National Institute of Nutrition.

Food allergy is the leading cause of anaphylactic shock outside of the hospital, accounting for an estimated 30,000 emergency room visits and 2,000 hospitalizations annually. It is estimated that 150 to 200 people die each year from food allergy reactions; approximately 50 people die annually from insect sting reactions.

When it comes to food allergies, eight foods account for 90 percent of the allergic reactions:
- Peanuts
- Tree nuts (walnuts, pecans, cashews, etc.)
- Shellfish
- Eggs
- Fish
- Milk
- Soy
- Wheat

Peanuts are the leading cause of severe allergic reactions, followed by shellfish, tree nuts and eggs.

A food allergy is an immune system response to a food that the body mistakenly believes is harmful. Once the immune system decides that a particular food is harmful, it creates specific antibodies to it. The next time the person eats the food, the immune system releases massive amounts of chemicals, including histamine, in order to protect the body. These chemicals trigger a cascade of allergic symptoms that can affect the respiratory system, gastrointestinal tract, skin or cardiovascular system. In the most severe cases, anaphylactic shock can result. Epinephrine, also called adrenaline, is the medication of choice for controlling a severe reaction. The drug is available by prescription in a quick-inject pen that can be self-administered.

For the millions of North Americans suffering from food allergies, there is help but no cure. Avoiding the suspect food is the easiest way to prevent an allergic reaction. Although an individual could be allergic to any food, such as fruits, vegetables and meats, allergies to those foods are not as common as to the eight foods listed above.

Milk allergy is relatively common among those with food allergies, although its effects are not usually as severe as allergies to shellfish, nuts and eggs. There is also a great deal of confusion and misinformation about milk allergy and lactose intolerance.

This book has been designed to help anyone with a milk allergy or lactose intolerance begin and maintain a dairy- or lactose-free diet. We will explain what a milk allergy is and how it differs from lactose intolerance; then we will describe the different symptoms and how to follow a dairy- and lactose-free diet. We will look at foods that can replace dairy products and give helpful tips for getting enough calcium and protein in your diet without using dairy products. We've included handy hints for eating out as well as cooking and preparing dairy-free recipes.

The recipes in this book can be classified into two types: those that have been adapted to be dairy-free, and recipes that have traditionally, and deliciously, been dairy-free. So in addition to learning how to make some of your favorite dishes dairy-free, we'll introduce you to wonderful dishes from around the world that stand on their own merit, no dairy needed or wanted.

If you have any concerns about following a dairy-free diet or have a condition such as pregnancy or lactation that may be affected by what you choose to eat, please consult your health-care provider before starting any diet.

So what is a milk allergy?

An allergy is an abnormal reaction by the immune system to a specific substance, called an allergen. An allergy to milk is caused by a reaction to proteins in milk, such as casein.

And lactose intolerance?

Lactose intolerance is an inability to digest lactose fully. Lactose is the primary carbohydrate in milk. Lactose is digested by the enzyme lactase. If the lactose is not broken down properly by lactase, components of the lactose remain in the intestinal tract, where it feeds bacteria, which then multiply, causing the characteristic symptoms of lactose intolerance, which include digestive-tract distress in the form of cramps, flatulence and/or diarrhea.

Sometime between weaning and young adulthood, many people begin losing their ability to produce lactase, the enzyme responsible for digesting lactose. Having a milk allergy or a deficiency in producing lactase doesn't mean you can't drink milk or eat other dairy products. Some sensitivity to milk is dose-related, with symptoms more likely to occur if milk is consumed frequently, if it is consumed in large amounts, or depending on what other dairy products are consumed with it. Many people who are lactose-intolerant are able to digest small amounts of dairy, thanks to friendly intestinal bacteria.

Lactose intolerance occurs in four forms: primary, secondary, congenital and galactosaemia. Primary lactose intolerance is a complete lack of lactase production, rather than diminished production; it tends to occur in early adolescence and stays throughout life.

Secondary lactose intolerance is usually short term and occurs if the lining in the intestines has become damaged as a result of illness or infection. Diarrhea and some medicines such as nonsteroidal anti-inflammatories, antibiotics and aspirin can inhibit lactase production for a few weeks.

Congenital lactose intolerance occurs in children born with no lactase production. These children cannot tolerate any amount of milk or milk products.

Galactosaemia is a rare hereditary disease and prevents the person with the ailment from metabolizing galactose, a component of lactose.

Allergy symptoms

Food allergy symptoms can range from a tingling sensation in the mouth to swelling of the tongue and throat, difficulty breathing, hives, vomiting, abdominal cramps, diarrhea, drop in blood pressure, loss of consciousness and death. Food allergy symptoms typically appear within minutes to two hours after the person has eaten the food to which he or she is allergic.

Food allergy symptoms appear in three categories: skin reactions; stomach and intestinal reactions; and nose, throat and lung reactions. The following symptoms are *not* specific to a milk allergy—they indicate an immune-system reaction to *any* allergen. If any of these symptoms persist *after* eliminating milk from your diet, consult a professional health-care provider who can help you identify any other allergies that you might have.

Skin reactions:
- Itchy, red rash
- Hives
- Eczema
- Swollen lips, tongue, mouth, face and/or throat
- Allergic eyes, black eyes ("shiners")

Stomach and intestinal reactions:
- Abdominal pain
- Abdominal bloating
- Gas or wind
- Cramps
- Diarrhea (usually very runny)
- Vomiting

Nose, throat and lung reactions:
- Coughing
- Wheezing
- Runny nose
- Sneezing
- Watery or itchy eyes
- Shortness of breath

Lactose-intolerance symptoms

The symptoms of lactose intolerance can resemble some of the stomach and intestinal reactions experienced as a result of milk or other food allergies. These symptoms include:
- Abdominal pain and bloating
- Stomach cramps
- Cramps
- Gas or wind

- Diarrhea (starting ½ to 2 hours after lactose consumption)
- Nausea and vomiting

Usually there is a correlation between the amount of lactose consumed and the severity of the symptoms. Someone suffering severe lactose intolerance could also experience malnutrition and weight loss.

Diagnosis

If you suspect you are allergic to milk or are lactose intolerant, you should have your health-care provider confirm a diagnosis. A blood test will verify an allergy; breath and stool tests will determine if you are lactose intolerant.

Once diagnosed, you may wish to consult with a registered dietitian or nutritional therapist. With a thorough health and lifestyle history, and by keeping a food and symptoms diary, your dietitian or therapist will be able to help you decide which foods, if any, might need to be reduced, substituted or eliminated from your diet. Never reduce, substitute or eliminate foods from a child's diet without professional advice.

Treatment

If you have a milk allergy, you will want to begin eating a diet that is milk-free and contains no milk products. As soon as you start to eat fewer foods containing the milk protein casein, and other triggers, your allergy symptoms should improve. If your allergy resulted from a weakened immune system, your symptoms may fade as your immune system becomes stronger. Generally, though, the treatment for a food allergy means eliminating the offending food long term.

If you have lactose intolerance, you may find that you can alleviate your symptoms by simply taking one of a number of products containing lactase that are available over the counter. The products, such as Lactaid™ and Dairy Ease™, provide the missing lactase enzyme needed to digest lactose. They can either be added to milk in droplet form or be taken with a meal or beverage as capsules.

What is a dairy-free diet?

A dairy-free diet excludes any food or product that is made with animal's milk. Strictly speaking, this is not just cow's milk but goat's and sheep's milk too. Milk-based foods include cream, butter, yogurt, cheese, cottage cheese, ice cream, milk chocolate and, in some cases, margarine.

Less obvious milk derivatives used by food manufacturers include whey, the thin fluid remnants of cheese making; casein, a milk protein; and lactose, a milk carbohydrate. These milk derivatives are often added to store-bought breads, cereals, sandwich spreads, salad dressings, cakes, cookies and fresh or frozen prepared meals.

If you have been diagnosed with a milk allergy or lactose intolerance, the first thing you need to do is learn to read labels. Until legislation governing food labels in the United States is simplified, you'll have to become something of a food detective. The following list of off-limits foods should help you avoid any milk or milk derivatives:

- Artificial butter flavor
- Butter, butter fat, butter oil
- Buttermilk
- Casein (casein hydrolysate)

- Caseinates (in all forms)
- Cheese
- Cottage cheese
- Cream
- Curds
- Custard
- Ghee (clarified butter used in Indian cooking)
- Half & half
- Lactalbumin, lacta albumin phosphate
- Lactulose
- Milk (in all forms, including condensed, derivative, dry, evaporated, goat's milk and milk from other animals, low-fat, malted, milkfat, non-fat, powder, protein, skimmed, solids, whole)
- Nougat
- Pudding
- Rennet casein
- Sour cream, sour cream solids
- Sour milk solids
- Whey (in all forms)
- Yogurt

The following may contain milk protein:
- Caramel candies
- Chocolate
- Flavorings (including natural and artificial)
- High-protein flour
- Lactic acid starter culture
- Lactose
- Luncheon meat, hot dogs, sausages
- Margarine
- Non-dairy products

The above list is available on a sturdy, wallet-sized plastic card from the Food Allergy & Anaphylaxis Network (FAAN). The card can be ordered by calling (800) 929-4040 or visiting www.foodallergy.org. The price is $2.00.

In Canada, a list of programs and services for adults and kids is available at Anaphylaxis Canada's website: www.anaphylaxis.org.

If a food does not have a label, the person with a milk allergy should not eat that food. If the label contains unfamiliar terms, the shopper should call the manufacturer and ask for detailed information about the ingredients, or avoid eating that food.

In addition to the above list, be aware that there are some unexpected sources of dairy. These include:
- Deli meat slicers, which are frequently used for both meat and cheese products.
- Some brands of canned tuna fish that contain casein, a milk protein.
- Many non-dairy products that contain casein (a milk derivative), listed on the ingredient labels.

- Some meats that may contain casein as a binder. Check all labels carefully.
- Many restaurants that put butter on steaks after they have been grilled to add extra flavor. The butter is not visible after it melts.

Don't despair!

The lists and "don'ts" might at first look overwhelming, but don't despair. Fortunately, milk is a very easy ingredient to substitute for in most cooking and baking, plus there are many delicious and healthful milk substitutes such as lactose-free milk, soy milk, rice milk and nut milks available at supermarkets and health food stores.

Although people with milk allergies will not be able to use sheep's or goat's milk, there are some chemical differences between goat's and cow's milk, and some people with lactose intolerance have found that they can tolerate goat's milk. This is probably due to the fact that casein, one of the milk proteins, occurs in different forms, and the one most prevalent in cow's milk is absent in goat's milk. The casein in goat's milk also groups together in smaller clusters, making it easier to tolerate.

Sheep's milk might also be tolerated by those with lactose intolerance who cannot eat cow's milk and its derivatives. Sheep's milk is available fresh and powdered. Buffalo mozzarella, however, should probably be avoided. In the U.S. and Canada, it is most likely made from cow's milk, not buffalo's milk, as it is in Italy. However, buffalo are in the bovine family, so buffalo mozzarella should be avoided if you have a milk allergy, although it might be all right if you have lactose intolerance.

People who are lactose-intolerant can sometimes eat yogurt. This is because the bacteria culture added to milk to turn it into yogurt breaks down some of the lactose before it is eaten. You'll have to experiment to see if cow, sheep or goat yogurt works best for you. Anyone with a milk allergy should avoid yogurt.

Hard cheeses can also sometimes be tolerated by people who are lactose intolerant because much of the lactose is removed during production. Aged Gouda and Edam cheeses and cottage cheese have the least amount of lactose.

What about kosher food?

Observant Jews use a system of product markings to indicate whether a food is kosher, or prepared in accordance with Jewish dietary rules. There are two kosher symbols that can be of help to those with a milk allergy: a "D," or the word dairy, on a label next to "K" or "U" (usually found near the product name) indicates presence of milk protein, and a "DE" on a label indicates the food was produced on equipment shared with dairy.

If the product contains neither meat nor dairy products, it is pareve (parev, parve). Pareve-labeling indicates that the products are considered milk-free according to religious specifications. Be aware that under Jewish law, a food product may be considered pareve even if it contains a very small amount of milk. Therefore, a product labeled as pareve could potentially have enough milk protein in it to cause a reaction in a person with a milk allergy.

Substituting with soy

Fortunately, milk is one of the most easily substituted ingredients in cooking and baking. You can easily modify existing recipes by substituting water or fruit juice measure for measure for milk.

In addition to water or juice, there are many excellent dairy-free ingredients that can replace milk. These include soy milk and cream, rice milk and nut and seed milks. In terms of availability, taste, appearance and nutrition, plain soy milk fortified with calcium (not calcium carbonate) is probably the closest approximation to milk, containing about the same amount of protein and calcium. It also has milk's creamy color and consistency.

But first, a little background on soy. It is a member of the legume family that has been cultivated for human consumption for thousands of years. Unlike most other legumes, soy is relatively low in carbohydrates and high in protein. Soy is the only member of the bean family that contains all eight essential amino acids. Although relatively high in fat compared with other beans, soybeans are cholesterol free, and the fat is mostly unsaturated, resulting in less of a potential concern about cholesterol buildup associated with animal foods such as dairy and meat. In addition, soy milk is thought to contain valuable plant estrogens that are linked to reduced rates of breast and prostate cancers, and it is a good source of Omega 3 fatty acids, the "good" fat that has been shown to reduce the risk of heart attack and stroke. It is also a good source of iron and B vitamins.

Soybeans are eaten fresh, boiled, sprouted, and dried and roasted. In addition, they are pressed into oil and made into a multitude of further-processed foods including tofu, a traditional Asian food made from ground soybeans that have been curdled and pressed into blocks like cheese. Soybeans also form the bases of soy cheese, soy yogurt, soy sour cream, soy ice cream, soy margarine, soy mayonnaise, soy flour, soy nut butter, soy sauce, textured vegetable protein, soy burgers, soy sausage and miso, a fermented soybean paste.

Rice milk is similar in appearance to milk and soy milk, but it contains less protein and calcium and has a milder flavor. Like soy milk, it is available at most supermarkets. Nut and seed milks can be used like milk but provide minimal calcium. Blanched almonds, cashews and sesame seeds make the best nut milks. A tablespoon of flaxseed ground with the nuts or a teaspoon of lecithin granules mixed with water will help blend the mixture to help keep the fats and liquid in suspension. Pour the nut milk through a strainer to remove any coarse pieces that could make the liquid grainy. Nut milks are available at natural foods stores.

But before adding any new food such as soy foods, soy milk or nut and seed milks to your diet, check with your health-care provider, registered dietitian or nutritional therapist. Some people are allergic to nuts and soy. Like milk, allergies to soy are generally not as severe as those to shellfish, tree nuts and eggs.

If you are not allergic to soy, a wide array of soy foods are available at supermarkets, natural foods stores and ethnic markets. As with any new product, read the label carefully. While soy itself is dairy-free, other ingredients may have been added to packaged products during processing.

The calcium question
Because milk and milk products such as yogurt are high in calcium, it is often thought that a dairy-free diet will leave people with low or inadequate amounts of this important mineral in their diet. In fact, calcium is quite common in food. What is important is the amount of calcium that is absorbed and retained by our bodies.

Calcium is used for building and maintaining healthy bones and teeth, as well as being necessary for muscle contraction, transmission and interpretation of nerve impulses and maintenance of cell membranes. Inadequate calcium has been linked to deformed bones, retarded growth and bone thinning, the precursor to osteoporosis.

Calcium is especially important during the years when bones grow larger and heavier. Pregnant and lactating women must also eat adequate amounts to help fetal bones calcify and produce mother's milk, while keeping their own bones strong.

In the Western diet, the current daily recommended amount for calcium is 1,000 mg, with the elderly and pregnant and lactating women needing even more. However, in countries where there is not a strong tradition of dairy and red meat consumption, people do very well on calcium levels of around 300 mg a day.

There are two reasons for the disparity in calcium levels in the Asian and Western diets. One reason is the absorption or malabsorption of calcium in our bodies; the other reason is the amount of calcium leeched from our bodies. Both malabsorption and leeching are effected by the foods we eat. In Asian diets, where far less animal protein in the form of dairy and red meat is consumed, people eat less calcium in their diet but absorb more of it. In the Western diet, high in dairy and red meat, we eat more calcium but do not efficiently absorb or utilize it. The primary culprit in calcium loss is protein, something the average American eats far too much of.

When too much animal protein is eaten, excess nitrogen and sulfur are produced in the blood, leading to an acid condition. To neutralize the acid, calcium is leeched from the bones and then excreted in the urine. Leeching is also caused by foods and drinks high in phosphorus. These include items processed with sodium phosphates and carbonated soft drinks. Foods containing oxalic acid, such as spinach, also decease absorption. Diets extremely high in fiber from whole grains containing phytic acid can also cause calcium to bind up, deceasing its absorption.

There are four simple steps you can take to ensure that you are getting adequate amounts of calcium: eat moderate, not excessive, amounts of animal protein; spend a little time in sunlight each day to get vitamin D, which helps utilize calcium; eat a variety of plant foods containing calcium; and add calcium supplements to your diet, if necessary.

If you have any concerns about the amount or sources of calcium in your diet, or whether you are absorbing it properly or need to use supplements, consult with your health-care provider, registered dietitian or nutritional therapist.

The table below lists various dairy-free foods and their calcium content.

Food	Calcium content mg per 3½ ounces
Oatmeal	52
All-purpose flour	130–140
Tomato sauce	48
Watercress, raw	170
Spinach, raw	170
Celery, raw	41
Garbanzo beans, cooked	43
Baked beans	53
Shrimp	150
Mussels	200
Anchovies	300
Sardines	300
Apricots	73
Oranges	47
Tahini	680
Egg	57

The protein paradox

Foods such as meat, fish and milk are prized for their high protein content, but the reality is that Western diets are rarely short of protein. In recent years the recommended daily amount for protein has been downgraded, and it is currently set at an average of about 45 grams per day. Some nutritionists recommend even lower amounts, closer to 30 to 35 grams per day, believing that animal protein and its associated cholesterol, saturated fat and undesirable Omega 6 fatty acids are responsible for a host of health problems, especially heart disease.

Because milk and its derivatives are often relied upon as a source of protein, it is important to make sure that the dairy-free diet provides enough protein. Fortunately, this is easy to accomplish using a rich variety of vegetable sources of protein such as soy foods, beans and legumes, along with moderate amounts of lean red meat, skinless poultry and seafood.

Anyone choosing a strict vegetarian diet that eschews all forms of animal food, including milk, cheese, yogurt, eggs, meat, poultry and seafood, should consult with a health-care professional to discuss their daily protein needs as well as the need to supplement their diet with B12 and other important vitamins and minerals.

Eating out

Eating out with a food allergy or a severe intolerance can at times be stressful. However, with a little forethought, patience and a simple explanation, you should be able to make your needs known with a minimum of fuss. A sense of humor helps as well.

If at all possible, call the restaurant ahead of time and explain to the manager or host that you have an allergy or severe intolerance. Ask what dishes on the menu are dairy-free. As eclectic and multi-ethnic as menus are today, chances are there are dishes made without dairy already listed. If a dish you would like to order contains dairy, ask the manager, hosts or chef if it is possible for the dish to be modified with non-dairy ingredients. If your menu questions are answered satisfactorily, make a reservation at the restaurant, giving the chef time to think about a dish and modify it, if necessary. Call the restaurant before your reservation to remind the staff that you are arriving and have special dietary needs. Do not call the restaurant during prime service hours and expect to speak to the chef. Instead, call during off hours and start with the manager or host.

If you do not have the opportunity to check out the restaurant or menu in advance, mention to the manager or host on the way to your table that you have a food allergy or severe intolerance. Ask if there is a server who is familiar with allergies, or a server who can answer detailed food questions, such as those concerning ingredients. Ask the server to point out to you menu items that are dairy-free. If the server seems unsure, ask to speak to the manager. During peak service hours, it is unlikely that the chef will be able to leave the kitchen to speak with you. Taking a moment to quietly explain your allergy to the manager or server will achieve better results than being fussy, difficult or loud. Please keep in mind that when restaurants are "slammed" with hungry diners during peak service hours, your special request puts extra strain on an already stressed kitchen and staff. If at all possible, make your needs known in advance, by telephone, during off-peak serving hours.

The restaurant you choose can also lessen the pitfalls of eating out. If the restaurant is French or Continental, you can assume that the sauces are cream and/or butter based. At an Italian restaurant, while there are still cream-based sauces, you will have a larger selection of tomato-based sauces. If you choose a Japanese, Thai or Chinese restaurant, you will likely find a large selection of dairy-free dishes.

At a French-style restaurant, you can order your dish with no sauce, or ask for the meat or fish to be grilled with oil instead of butter. In general, chefs tend to respond better to a specific request, such as "no sauce or butter, please," rather than a blanket "no dairy."

In Indian restaurants, most dishes are cooked in ghee, which is butter that has been clarified to remove most of the milk solids. While ghee is still off limits for people with milk allergies, many people with lactose intolerance find that they can eat ghee. Indian dishes might also contain yogurt, which many people with lactose intolerance can eat, although people with milk allergies should not.

When it comes to fast food, pizzas can be ordered with just the tomato sauce and other dairy-free toppings such as pepperoni, mushrooms, olives or pineapple.

Other reasons to be dairy-free

Not all people choose to be dairy-free as a result of allergies or intolerance. They choose a dairy-free diet for health reasons; for weight loss; for ethical reasons such as opposition to animal cruelty; for environmental reasons such as the wasteful use of water to grow grain to feed animals or the pollution resulting from factory farming techniques. Some people just don't feel quite right and suspect that dairy foods may be the cause; others prefer to avoid using products that might contain traces of the growth hormones and antibiotics that are routinely used to treat cows. Still others avoid meat and dairy products out of concern over mad cow disease.

For whatever reason you choose to eliminate dairy from your diet, the result can benefit your health, and the health of the planet, in many ways.

- *Lower cholesterol and fat intake:* High levels of cholesterol and fat in milk have been linked to heart disease, stroke and other circulatory diseases.
- *Fewer mucus problems:* Congestion, hay fever, and sinus problems often occur where there is high dairy consumption. This is because milk tends to produce mucus in the intestines and other parts of the body.
- *Better protein digestion:* Milk neutralizes stomach acids, and since proteins are digested in the acid stomach environment, this results in proteins being only partially digested, often causing discomfort.
- *Better nutrient absorption:* Milk tends to build up mucus in the intestines, and when it mixes with food residue it forms a hard material coating the intestinal wall. This blocks movement through the intestinal wall, affecting both nutrient absorption and enzyme secretion that aids digestion. Excluding dairy from your diet will also discourage "unfriendly" bacteria that inhibit mineral absorption from colonizing in your intestines.
- *Healthier cells, potassium balance:* Our bodies have a mechanism to maintain the correct balance of potassium and sodium ions within our cells. It is known as the sodium-potassium pump and works to drive the sodium ions out while holding on to the potassium ions and keeping cells healthy. In babies the requirements in the cell are reversed, and milk has the capability of encouraging sodium into the cells against the force of the sodium-potassium pump. As the baby changes into a child, the body requires less intracellular sodium. By continuing to drink milk, too much sodium enters the cells, causing increased susceptibility to chronic disease.
- *Healthier cells, magnesium balance:* Despite containing high levels of calcium, milk and milk products can actually deplete the body of calcium. This is because magnesium is needed to regulate calcium metabolism and keep the body's calcium in the right places,

such as the bones. Milk contains a low ratio of magnesium to calcium (1=10). Unless we eat foods with high levels of magnesium to counteract the low level of magnesium in milk, we cannot utilize the calcium properly. A dairy-free diet will help you achieve a better calcium-magnesium ratio.

- *Less colic in babies:* Studies have shown that bottle-fed babies with colic tend to improve if dairy is removed from their diets. Lactating mothers who eat and drink dairy products pass along cow's proteins and antibodies to their babies, also causing colic.
- *Healthier arteries:* By skipping dairy you will avoid the enzyme xanthine oxidase in milk, which is believed to attack the coronary arteries. The enzyme is a particular concern in homogenized milk.
- *Other concerns:* Increasing research is finding links between diseases and dairy consumption. Some of these concerns include insulin-dependent diabetes, autism, hyperactivity, learning difficulties, insomnia, pulmonary disease and eczema.

Healthy eating and living
Dairy-free or not, the general guidelines for healthy eating remain the same: low-fat, no added salt, at least five portions of fresh vegetables and fruits a day, and replacement of refined foods with whole-grain versions whenever possible.

And don't neglect exercise as part of your plan for healthy eating and living. Too many calories, no matter how good they are for you, are still too many calories and will result in unwanted extra pounds. Extra weight, even a relatively small amount, is associated with a number of chronic diseases.

Cooking and preparing recipes
If you pick up a cookbook and find a recipe that you would like to make, but it includes dairy products, don't feel that you can't make it. As you get used to your new dairy-free way of eating, you will find that you are easily able to spot substitutions. There are a few basic replacements that will make your life easier, such as replacing butter with dairy-free margarine for spreading, frying or baking. In many cases, a mild-flavored oil such as canola or olive can be used to replace butter. Try the many milk substitutes such as soy milk, rice milk and nut and seed milks with different recipes.

You will see that hummus has been added to a number of recipes. It creates a creamy feel and texture without adding dairy. Soy yogurt and soy sour cream can also be experimented with.

If you are cooking for someone who has a milk allergy or lactose intolerance, *do not* experiment on them. If you are in doubt about any ingredient, check with the person first. It is not worth risking any possible harm or discomfort to another person.

If you do not already have one, a blender, food processor or wand (immersion) blender is a worthwhile investment, as the texture of almost any pureed food can add a creamy look and feel to many dishes.

Unless otherwise noted, all recipes have been made with medium eggs, and all measures are level. The nutritional data are based on the lower number of servings indicated, if a range is given, and the first ingredient listed where an alternative is mentioned. Optional and "to taste" ingredients are not included in the nutritional data. In the list of ingredients, North American measurements are given in the left-hand column and metric in the right-hand; in many cases, exact conversions were not possible.

The information contained in this book is correct at the time of writing and is intended as a general reference only. It is not suitable for professional medical advice or as a substitution for a medical exam. Always seek the advice of your health-care provider if you believe you are suffering from the symptoms of a milk allergy or lactose intolerance, or any other medical condition. No information in this book should be used to diagnose, treat, cure or prevent a dairy allergy or lactose intolerance or any other medical condition without the supervision of a health-care provider.

Food Allergy & Anaphylaxis Network (U.S.)

Via Mail
10400 Eaton Place, Suite 107
Fairfax, VA 22030-2208

Via Phone
(800) 929-4040

Via Fax
(703) 691-2713

Via Email
faan@foodallergy.org

Anaphylaxis Canada

Via Mail
416 Moore Avenue, Suite 306
Toronto, ON M4G1C9

Via Phone
(416) 785-5666

Via Fax
(416) 785-0458

Via Email and Internet
info@anaphylaxis.ca
www.anaphylaxis.org

Additional information (also see "Helpful Organizations," page 195)

For a list of doctors in your area, please contact one of the following organizations:

United States

American Academy of Allergy, Asthma & Immunology
(800) 822-ASMA
www.aaaai.org

American College of Allergy, Asthma & Immunology
(800) 842-7777
www.allergy.mcg.edu

American Academy of Pediatrics
(800) 433-9016
www.aap.org

Canada

College of Family Physicians of Canada
(905) 629-0900
www.cfpc.ca

Dietitians of Canada
(416) 596-0857
www.dietitians.ca

National Institute of Nutrition
(613) 235-3355
www.nin.ca

—*Miller Rogers and Emily White*

Soups, Dips, Starters and Snacks

Chunky Leek, Potato and Lentil Soup

Cream of Spinach and Nutmeg Soup

Smoked Trout Chowder

Creamy Carrot and Cilantro Soup

*Miso Soup with Tofu, Noodles
and Wakame Seaweed*

Hummus Dip

Chive Cream Cheese Dip

Tahini and Lemon Dip

Herbed Olive and Tuna Dip

Avocado and Shrimp Empañadas

Crab Cakes

Crispy Garlic- and Leek-Stuffed Mussels

Seafood Fritto Misto

Herb-Crumbed Catfish Fillets

Niçoise Tartlets

Smoked Salmon Roulade with Smoked Trout Mousse

Squid with Chilies and Tomatoes

Chinese-Style Crispy Pork Strips

Marinated Lime and Sesame Chicken Sticks

Smoked Duck Salad with Spiced Walnuts

Mushroom and Nut Pâté

Roasted Cherry Tomato Bruschetta

Crispy Spinach and Pine Nut Filo Parcels

Hummus, Chili and Crisp Vegetable Wrap

Bacon, Tomato and Watercress Wrap

Never cook legumes in salted water. They will become tough. Try this recipe using red lentils or brown lentils, varying the cooking time accordingly.

Garam masala is an Indian spice that may be found in ethnic aisles or at Indian grocery stores.

Chunky Leek, Potato and Lentil Soup

Serves 4–6

Lentils are easy to cook and do not require pre-soaking. They also provide an excellent source of protein and fiber. I usually have plenty of onions, potatoes and lentils in my cupboard and quite often make this recipe when everything else has run out and I want a quick and nutritious soup for lunch.

1 cup	lentils (7 oz)	196 g
2	medium leeks	2
5/8 lb	potatoes (weight after peeling)	280 g
1 tbsp	sunflower oil	15 ml
1	large onion, finely chopped	1
3	cloves garlic, crushed	3
1 tsp	garam masala	1 tsp
1 1/2 qts	boiling water	1 1/2 liters
2–3 tbsps	vegan (dairy-free) bouillon	2–3 tbsps
	salt and freshly ground pepper	
1 tbsp	chopped fresh parsley	25 g

First rinse the lentils. Cover with plenty of cold water in a large saucepan. Bring this to a boil and simmer for 10 minutes, drain well.

Wash, trim and chop the leeks, and cut the potatoes into small cubes. Heat the oil in a large saucepan, and fry the onion and garlic for about 4 minutes until soft. Next add the garam masala and drained lentils and stir well.

Pour over the boiling water, and cook for a further 15 minutes.

Mix in the potatoes, leeks and bouillon powder, and cook this uncovered, stirring occasionally, for a further 10 minutes until soft but not mushy.

Season with salt and freshly ground pepper.

Spoon the soup into warmed bowls, and sprinkle with chopped parsley.

PER SERVING	
Calories	291
% Calories from fat	13
Fat (g)	4.3
Saturated fat (g)	0.4
Cholesterol (mg)	0
Sodium (mg)	506
Protein (g)	16
Carbohydrate (g)	49.3
Calcium (mg)	82.4
EXCHANGES	
Milk	0.0
Vegetable	0.0
Fruit	0.0
Bread	3.0
Meat	1.0
Fat	0.5

This soup can also be made with watercress and produces a wonderful nutritious dish.

Cream of Spinach and Nutmeg Soup

Serves 4–6

This should be a lovely fresh-looking green soup. To make it more impressive, pour a swirl of soy cream onto the top before serving. The less you cook the spinach, the more the color and nutrients are retained.

1 tbsp	vegetable oil	1 tbsp
1	large onion, roughly chopped	1
2	ribs celery, washed and chopped	2
4 cups	diced potatoes (weight after peeling 1lb)	450 g
1 qt	vegan vegetable stock	1 liter
5–6 cups	spinach (7 oz)	5–6 cups
1/4 tsp	freshly grated nutmeg	1/4 tsp
	salt and freshly ground pepper	

Heat a large saucepan with the oil. Gently cook the onion and celery for about 5 minutes until soft, taking care not to let them brown. Add the diced potato and stir well.

Pour in the stock, bring this up to a boil and simmer about 20 minutes until the potato is beginning to fall apart and the onion is tender. Wash the spinach well; remove any tough stalks but keep the tender ones.

Put the spinach in the pan and push down, cover with lid and allow to cook for about 4 minutes, with all spinach submerged. It should not be cooked for too long or the soup will become gray; cool slightly.

Purée in a blender or food processor until smooth and creamy. Season with nutmeg, salt and freshly ground pepper. To serve, heat the soup through gently.

PER SERVING	
Calories	172
% Calories from fat	23
Fat (g)	4.9
Saturated fat (g)	0.5
Cholesterol (mg)	0
Sodium (mg)	1077
Protein (g)	7.7
Carbohydrate (g)	28.7
Calcium (mg)	74

EXCHANGES	
Milk	0.0
Vegetable	0.0
Fruit	0.0
Bread	2.0
Meat	0.0
Fat	1.0

For a different variation, try this recipe with crab, clams or shrimp. Or for a vegan chowder, omit fish stock and use vegetable stock. The potato and sweetcorn alone provide a tasty, nourishing soup.

Smoked Trout Chowder

Serves 6

A chowder is a cream-based chunky fish soup that originated in North America. We often have this nourishing soup as a meal in itself. The potatoes should just be beginning to break down and slightly thicken the soup. The addition of sweetcorn is not only traditional, but it also provides added milkiness to the dish.

1	medium leek	1
1 tbsp	vegetable oil	1 tbsp
1	large onion, finely chopped	1
4 cups	cubed potatoes (weight after peeling 1 lb)	450 g
2½ cups	vegetable, fish or chicken stock	570 ml
1 lb	fillet of smoked trout, skinned, boned and cut into small cubes	450 g
1 cup	frozen, fresh or canned, drained, sweetcorn kernels (1 cup)	170 g
1 tbsp	arrowroot	1 tbsp
1¾ cups	coconut milk	400 ml
2 tbsps	chopped fresh cilantro to serve	2 tbsps

Wash, trim and thinly slice the leek. In a large pan, heat oil and gently cook the onion and leek for about 5 minutes until soft but not brown.

Add the potatoes and cook for about 3 minutes, stirring regularly. Pour in the stock, mix well and simmer for 20 minutes until the potatoes and leeks are both tender.

Add the cubed trout, sweetcorn and arrowroot (if using fresh corn off the cob, add to the soup after potatoes have been cooking for 5 minutes) and simmer for 5 minutes.

Pour in the coconut milk and warm through. Serve in warm bowls garnished with fresh cilantro.

PER SERVING	
Calories	370
% Calories from fat	47
Fat (g)	20.4
Saturated fat (g)	15.3
Cholesterol (mg)	24.9
Sodium (mg)	1200
Protein (g)	23.7
Carbohydrate (g)	27.4
Calcium (mg)	44.5

EXCHANGES	
Milk	0.0
Vegetable	0.0
Fruit	0.0
Bread	2.0
Meat	2.0
Fat	2.5

Use parsnips, cauliflower, broccoli or celery for a variation.

Creamy Carrot and Cilantro Soup

Serves 6–8

This rich, creamy soup is delicious as a lunch dish with hot crusty bread. It is also delicious with a sprinkling of crispy bacon and parsley on top instead of cilantro. This forms the basis of many creamy-style vegetable soups.

2 tsps	vegan margarine	16 g
1	large onion, chopped	1
3 cups	chopped potatoes (weight after peeling 10 oz)	280 g
4 cups	chopped carrots (weight after peeling 12 oz)	340 g
1½ qts	vegetable stock	1.5 liters
	small bunch fresh cilantro	

Melt margarine in a large saucepan over medium heat. Add the onion and gently cook for about 4 minutes until soft but not brown.

Stir in the chopped potatoes and carrots and pour the stock over. Bring the soup to a boil and gently simmer for about 30–40 minutes or until vegetables are soft.

Purée in a blender or food processor until smooth and creamy. Season with salt and freshly ground pepper.

Gently reheat. Serve the soup in hot bowls with freshly chopped cilantro sprinkled on top.

PER SERVING

Calories	112
% Calories from fat	18
Fat (g)	2.5
Saturated fat (g)	0.3
Cholesterol (mg)	0
Sodium (mg)	1041
Protein (g)	4.6
Carbohydrate (g)	21.3
Calcium (mg)	32.8

EXCHANGES

Milk	0.0
Vegetable	0.0
Fruit	0.0
Bread	1.5
Meat	0.0
Fat	0.0

This could also be made without noodles for a lighter soup. I included them to make it a little more substantial and therefore also suitable as a light meal.

Miso Soup with Tofu, Noodles and Wakame Seaweed

Serves 4

This soup is very nourishing and high in protein. Miso is readily available in health food shops. The wakame seaweed is widely used in Japanese soups and salads and has no calories. It is very high in minerals and calcium. Try experimenting with Japanese foods if you enjoy this soup.

1	piece dried wakame seaweed (about 4 inches)	10–15 g
1	pack firm tofu (about 10 oz)	280 g
1 qt	weak vegetable stock (could use fish stock)	1.2 liters
1 cup	medium or thin noodles (1 cup)	110 g
4 tsps	low-salt miso	4 tsps
2	green onions, trimmed and cut into fine rounds (save the green ends for garnish)	2

Soak wakame in cold water until it softens (about 10 minutes); don't oversoak. Drain and trim away any tough sections, then cut into 1-inch lengths.

Cut the tofu into $1/2$-inch cubes. Heat stock over medium heat until very hot, add noodles and cook for half their required cooking time (about 2 minutes).

Turn heat down and allow to cool slightly. Add the miso and stir well. Then stir in the green onions and tofu and allow the soup to heat through, but do not boil.

Lastly, add the wakame and remove from heat just before soup boils. Serve in pre-heated bowls garnished with the green ends of the onions.

PER SERVING	
Calories	188
% Calories from fat	22
Fat (g)	5
Saturated fat (g)	0.5
Cholesterol (mg)	0
Sodium (mg)	1275
Protein (g)	12.5
Carbohydrate (g)	27.3
Calcium (mg)	124
EXCHANGES	
Milk	0.0
Vegetable	0.0
Fruit	0.0
Bread	2.0
Meat	1.0
Fat	0.0

Try making this with soaked and cooked yellow split peas for an interesting alternative.

Hummus Dip

Serves 16 (1 heaping tablespoon per serving)

Hummus is a popular dip that originates in Lebanon. The texture is often deliciously creamy, yet the ingredients are all extremely nutritious. Hummus will store well for several weeks in the fridge, making it a useful food to have for quick nutritious snacks. Try using it in sandwiches with crisp salad or sprouted alfalfa.

Many supermarkets now stock hummus. However, making it at home is certainly more economical, and also you can monitor the salt content, as the bought product can be deceptively high in salt.

2	15-oz cans chick peas, drained (or 4 cups cooked from dried)	2
1/4 cup	tahini (puréed sesame seeds)	1/4 cup
	juice from 2–3 lemons	
3	cloves garlic	3
3 tbsps	olive oil	45 ml
2–3 tsps	salt	2–3 tsps
	paprika to garnish	

Blend the chick peas, tahini, lemon juice and garlic in a food processor until it has a creamy and smooth consistency.

Gradually add the olive oil; if mixture is too thick add water spoon by spoon until smooth-dropping consistency. Blend in the salt a teaspoon at a time, tasting for seasoning.

Spoon some into a serving dish and sprinkle the top with paprika if desired. Store the remaining hummus in sealed jars in the fridge. This recipe above makes about 3 jars (24 ounces) of hummus.

PER SERVING	
Calories	76
% Calories from fat	55
Fat (g)	4.8
Saturated fat (g)	0.6
Cholesterol (mg)	0
Sodium (mg)	367
Protein (g)	1.9
Carbohydrate (g)	7
Calcium (mg)	14.8

EXCHANGES	
Milk	0.0
Vegetable	0.0
Fruit	0.0
Bread	0.5
Meat	0.0
Fat	1.0

Try this served on small squares of pumpernickel as a smart canapé topped with smoked salmon, gravlax or mock caviar. Challenge anyone to guess it is dairy free.
  Also delicious as a dip with crudités.

PER SERVING	
Calories	68
% Calories from fat	83
Fat (g)	6.3
Saturated fat (g)	1.3
Cholesterol (mg)	0
Sodium (mg)	90
Protein (g)	0.7
Carbohydrate (g)	2.2
Calcium (mg)	1.7
EXCHANGES	
Milk	0.0
Vegetable	0.0
Fruit	0.0
Bread	0.0
Meat	0.0
Fat	1.5

Add Dijon mustard and use as a coleslaw dressing.

PER SERVING	
Calories	53
% Calories from fat	87
Fat (g)	5.4
Saturated fat (g)	0.6
Cholesterol (mg)	0
Sodium (mg)	44
Protein (g)	0.7
Carbohydrate (g)	1
Calcium (mg)	5.5
EXCHANGES	
Milk	0.0
Vegetable	0.0
Fruit	0.0
Bread	0.0
Meat	0.0
Fat	1.0

Chive Cream Cheese Dip

Serves 6 (2 tablespoons per serving)

Soy cream cheese can be bought from most health food shops and tastes very similar to normal cream cheese but actually contains less fat. By adding lemon and chives you can make a quick and easy dip, which will store well for up to a week.

1/2 cup	soy cream cheese	110 g
1/4 cup	soy cream	60 ml
2 tsps	lemon juice	10 ml
10	strands of chives, chopped	10

  Beat the soy cream cheese and soy cream together in a bowl until smooth.
  Add the lemon juice and chives, mixing well. Store in sealed container in the fridge until required. Makes about 3/4 cup.

Tahini and Lemon Dip

Serves 8 (1 tablespoon per serving)

This makes a smooth and creamy dip suitable for crudités. The tahini and other ingredients form a thick emulsion, so it can be used as a substitute for egg-based mayonnaise. Serve with crisp raw carrots, celery, cauliflower florets and cucumber sticks.

2 tbsps	tahini	2 tbsps
3 tbsps	water	45 ml
2 tbsps	mild oil (sunflower or vegetable)	30 ml
	juice of 1/2 lemon	
1 tsp	soy sauce	5 ml
1/2 tsp	honey (optional)	1/2 tsp

  Mix the tahini with half the water and whisk well until smooth. Continue whisking and gradually drizzle in the oil until the mixture thickens, then stir in the remaining water.
  Season with the lemon juice, soy sauce and honey. Chill in a sealed container until required. Makes about 1/2 cup.

Herbed Olive and Tuna Dip

Serves 10 (1 tablespoon per serving)

This is a Mediterranean-style dip that is full of flavor. Delicious served as a dip with crudités or on hot grilled toast.

1	5-oz can tuna, in water, drained	1
1/4 cup	pitted black olives	55 g
1	slice white bread, crusts removed	1
1	clove garlic, crushed	1
2 tbsps	capers, drained and rinsed	2 tbsps
2 tsps	wine vinegar	10 ml
1 tbsp	lemon juice	15 ml
2 tbsps	olive oil	30 ml
2 tbsps	low-fat mayonnaise (optional)	2 tbsps
2 tbsps	chopped parsley	2 tbsps
1 tsp	chopped fresh thyme leaves	1 tsp

Process the tuna, olives, bread, garlic, capers, vinegar and lemon juice until well combined.

While motor is running, drizzle in the olive oil until the mixture becomes smooth.

Finally, stir in mayonnaise, if using, and herbs and store in the fridge. Makes about 3/4 cup.

PER SERVING

Calories	57
% Calories from fat	58
Fat (g)	3.7
Saturated fat (g)	0.5
Cholesterol (mg)	4.2
Sodium (mg)	177
Protein (g)	3.9
Carbohydrate (g)	2.1
Calcium (mg)	13.6

EXCHANGES

Milk	0.0
Vegetable	0.0
Fruit	0.0
Bread	0.0
Meat	1.0
Fat	0.0

For vegetarians, try other fillings such as mushroom and eggplant. These could also be deep-fried for a light and crispy texture.

Avocado and Shrimp Empañadas

Serves 8

These crisp Mexican-style parcels are perfect to serve as a starter or a light main course with some crisp salad. They are delicious served with either the Tomato and Mint Salsa on page 120 or Roasted Sweetcorn and Lime Salsa on page 118.

1	beaten egg for glazing	1
1 tbsp	vegetable oil	15 ml
1	medium onion, finely chopped	1
2	cloves garlic, crushed	2
1	heaping teaspoon ground cumin	1
2 tbsps	tomato purée	2 tbsps
3	bottled jalapeño peppers, drained, chopped	3
1 tsp	dried oregano	1 tsp
2	medium tomatoes, quartered, seeds removed, chopped	2
³/₄ lb	cooked, peeled large shrimp (cut into thirds)	337 g
1	large, firm but ripe avocado or 2 smaller ones	1
	salt and freshly ground pepper	
1 recipe	Cornmeal Pastry on page 185	1 recipe
1	egg, beaten	1

Pre-heat the oven to 375F. Grease a large baking sheet.

Heat the oil in a large saucepan and gently fry the onion and garlic for about 5 minutes until soft. Stir in the ground cumin and cook for about 2 minutes. Mix in the tomato purée, peppers, oregano and chopped tomatoes.

Remove this mixture from the heat and allow to cool slightly before adding the shrimp and the peeled, diced avocado. Season well.

Divide the cornmeal pastry into 8 portions. Roll portions into 6-inch rounds.

Divide the filling and spoon onto the rounds; brush edges with beaten egg. Fold rounds in half, enclosing filling. Press edges together firmly, trim with knife and decorate edges with fork. Place the parcels onto the prepared baking sheet. Brush the pastry with beaten egg.

Bake in a hot oven for about 20 minutes until browned and heated through.

PER SERVING	
Calories	335
% Calories from fat	48
Fat (g)	18.1
Saturated fat (g)	3
Cholesterol (mg)	165
Sodium (mg)	478
Protein (g)	15.3
Carbohydrate (g)	28
Calcium (mg)	47.1

EXCHANGES	
Milk	0.0
Vegetable	0.0
Fruit	0.0
Bread	2.0
Meat	1.0
Fat	3.0

If using fresh whole crab, make sure you discard the small grayish-white stomach sac just behind the mouth and the long white-pointed "dead man's fingers." These can be easily distinguished, and it is a quick and easy job to remove them.

Crab Cakes

Serves 4 (1 cake each)

These crab cakes make an impressive starter or light main course with lemon dressing. The grated half-cooked potato holds the cakes together, unlike traditional fish cakes which use mashed potato to bind the fish and are coated in breadcrumbs. The result is a much lighter and tastier fish cake.

Try to use fresh crabmeat if possible; otherwise, defrosted frozen crabmeat would be a good alternative. Delicious served accompanied with the Creamy Lemon Dressing on page 140.

5–6	small boiling potatoes (10 oz)	280 g
10 oz	mixed fresh crabmeat (try and use mainly white crabmeat)	280 g
1 tbsp	chopped fresh dill	1 tbsp
2	green onions, finely chopped	2
	zest and juice of one large lemon	
1/2 tsp	cayenne pepper	1/2 tsp
	salt and freshly ground pepper	
	oil for frying	
	sprigs of fresh cilantro or parsley to garnish	

First peel the potatoes, then steam or boil them in boiling salted water for about 10 minutes. They should be slightly uncooked in the middle. Allow the potatoes to cool.

Shred the potatoes into a large bowl using a cheese grater. In another bowl, carefully mix together the crabmeat, dill, green onion, zest and juice of lemon with the seasonings.

Now carefully combine the grated potato with the crab mixture, mixing well without breaking up the potatoes too much.

Have a large baking sheet handy, and divide the mixture into four for a light main course. Squeeze each portion into a ball and then slightly flatten each ball into a small round cake. When the cakes are all made, cover with plastic wrap and refrigerate for 1–2 hours to become firmer.

To cook the crab cakes, heat a large frying pan (preferably non-stick) with 1 tablespoon of oil. When the oil is hot but not smoking, pan-fry the crab cakes for about 4 minutes, then turn the crab cakes carefully with a spatula, and repeat on the other side (depending on size) until heated through and golden.

Transfer to a warm serving plate. Garnish with cilantro or parsley.

PER SERVING	
Calories	134
% Calories from fat	9
Fat (g)	1.3
Saturated fat (g)	0.1
Cholesterol (mg)	37.5
Sodium (mg)	761
Protein (g)	16.2
Carbohydrate (g)	14.3
Calcium (mg)	60.2

EXCHANGES	
Milk	0.0
Vegetable	0.0
Fruit	0.0
Bread	1.0
Meat	2.0
Fat	0.0

Mussels are at their best in the cold weather, usually from October to March. A sign of freshness is that most when raw are tightly closed; if there are too many with open shells don't buy them. Buy extra to account for any that may be discarded. To wash, put in a sink full of cold water. First, throw away any that float to the top, then leave the tap running and scrape off barnacles with a knife, pulling off the hairy beards. Discard any broken mussels and those that are open and refuse to close tight when given a sharp tap with a knife. Once sorted and cleaned, place in a bowl of clean water. Once cooked, discard any whose shells haven't opened.

Crispy Garlic- and Leek-Stuffed Mussels

Serves 6

Mussels go very well cooked with leeks, which, combined with breadcrumbs and garlic, make a delicious starter. The dish may be prepared up to a day before, and the final broiling done just before serving. Serve with crusty fresh bread and a squeeze of fresh lemon.

	about 30 mussels	
1 cup	dry white wine (or stock if preferred)	240 ml
1	small onion, finely chopped	1
1	large leek	1
1 tbsp	olive oil	15 ml
4	cloves garlic, peeled and crushed	4
3–4 slices	crusty white bread	3–4 slices
1 tbsp	chopped fresh tarragon	1 tbsp
1	bunch of parsley, finely chopped	1
3 tbsps	vegan margarine	75 g
	more olive oil and wedges of lemon to garnish	

Begin by washing and scrubbing the mussels (see sidebar).

Pour the wine into a large pan with the chopped onion and bring this to a boil. Tip in the prepared mussels, and cover with a lid. After about 4 minutes, shake pan to ensure that the mussels are moved about.

The mussels are cooked when they have all opened up, which should take about 8 minutes altogether. Remove the pan from the heat and allow to cool. Next, clean and chop the leek finely, discarding any tough outer leaves.

In a large frying pan, heat the olive oil and gently cook the leek and garlic, stirring occasionally, for about 5 minutes until soft but not brown. Tip into a large bowl and allow to cool slightly. Process the bread into crumbs.

When leek mixture is slightly cool, add the tarragon, parsley and breadcrumbs, mixing thoroughly.

Stir in the margarine and press the mixture together with a spoon. Season with salt and pepper.

Open the mussels, leaving one half-shell with the mussel inside, discarding the other half-shell which will be empty.

PER SERVING	
Calories	229
% Calories from fat	41
Fat (g)	10.4
Saturated fat (g)	1.8
Cholesterol (mg)	20
Sodium (mg)	379
Protein (g)	10.9
Carbohydrate (g)	16.8
Calcium (mg)	77.2

EXCHANGES	
Milk	0.0
Vegetable	0.0
Fruit	0.0
Bread	1.0
Meat	1.0
Fat	2.0

Using your hands, stuff the mixture into the mussel shell, smoothing down and covering the mussel completely. Place on a large tray.

Either store stuffed mussels in fridge for use within 2 days or to cook; place under a hot broiler for about 5 minutes until golden and crispy.

Drizzle with some more olive oil and serve garnished with lemon wedges.

Try to use a fairly good quality vegetable or peanut oil. The fish is also good if it is fried in a mild-flavored light olive oil.

Seafood Fritto Misto

Serves 8–10 as starter

Fritto Misto originated in Italy, where there are many different versions. In some cases a yeast or beer batter is made to coat the fish or shellfish. The version below is much more straightforward and, providing fresh shellfish is used, equally as delicious. Serve hot with mayonnaise mixed with a squeeze of lemon and some salad.

1/2 lb	peeled shrimp	225 g
1/2 lb	small squid (buy ready cleaned)	225 g
1/2 lb	haddock or mahi-mahi	225 g
	plenty of all-purpose flour for dusting	
	oil for deep-frying	
	salt and freshly ground pepper	
	lemon wedges and parsley to garnish	

Remove veins from the back of shrimp if necessary, and cut in half lengthways.

Cut the squid into rings and pat dry using absorbent paper. Wash the haddock and dry thoroughly. On a large plate, dust all the seafood with plenty of flour, shaking off any surplus.

Heat the oil in large saucepan or a deep-fat fryer. To determine whether the oil is hot enough for frying, drop a tiny amount of fish into the oil: it should stiffen and instantly come to the surface.

Deep-fry the seafood in hot oil, a few pieces at a time, until it has formed a rich, golden crust on one side; using a slotted spoon, turn the seafood over to cook the other side.

Remove from the oil, drain on absorbent paper and season with salt and pepper.

Serve hot garnished with wedges of lemon and sprigs of fresh parsley.

PER SERVING	
Calories	80
% Calories from fat	13
Fat (g)	1.1
Saturated fat (g)	0.2
Cholesterol (mg)	124.3
Sodium (mg)	69
Protein (g)	15.4
Carbohydrate (g)	1.1
Calcium (mg)	31.1
EXCHANGES	
Milk	0.0
Vegetable	0.0
Fruit	0.0
Bread	0.0
Meat	2.0
Fat	0.0

Herb-Crumbed Catfish Fillets

Serves 4

Ideal as a starter or light supper. Serve with a spoonful of warmed Roasted Tomato Sauce on page 119.

4	fresh catfish fillets (about 1 lb)	4
	all-purpose flour	
	salt and freshly ground pepper	
1	egg, beaten	1
2 tbsps	soy milk	30 ml
1 cup	breadcrumbs	220 g
1 tbsp	finely chopped parsley	1 tbsp
1 tbsp	finely chopped oregano	1 tbsp
	peanut oil for shallow frying	
	lemon wedges to garnish	

Rinse catfish and scrape off any loose scales. Fillet by using a sharp knife and beginning at tail. Cut down against backbone until you reach the head, cutting off fillet at that point. Repeat on the other side, and tidy the fillets up pulling out larger pin bones.

Alternatively, ask the fish market to fillet the fish for you.
To coat the fillets you will need 3 large plates. On the first plate season the flour with salt and freshly ground pepper. On the second plate mix the beaten egg with the soy milk. And on the third, combine the breadcrumbs with the fresh herbs.

Dip each fillet first in the seasoned flour, then the beaten egg and finally roll them in the breadcrumbs.

Place fillets on a tray sprinkled with a few of the breadcrumbs to stop them from sticking together.

In a large frying pan, pour about 2 tablespoons of peanut oil. When hot, fry several fillets at a time for about 3 minutes until golden brown. Turn over and repeat on the other side. Keep these warm while you cook the remaining fillets. You may need to wipe out the pan with paper towels to remove any burnt crumbs before adding another 2 tablespoons of oil. Serve on a warm serving platter garnished with lemon wedges.

PER SERVING	
Calories	281
% Calories from fat	37
Fat (g)	11.4
Saturated fat (g)	2.7
Cholesterol (mg)	106
Sodium (mg)	310
Protein (g)	22.8
Carbohydrate (g)	20
Calcium (mg)	83
EXCHANGES	
Milk	0.0
Vegetable	0.0
Fruit	0.0
Bread	1.5
Meat	2.0
Fat	1.0

Change the filling if you are cooking for a vegan. Omit the anchovies and the tuna and use marinated artichoke hearts, peppers or mushrooms.

Niçoise Tartlets

Serves 6

These tartlets have a wonderful Mediterranean theme. I tend to keep most of the ingredients in my cupboard and often have puff pastry in the freezer, thus making it a great and impressive dish for an unexpected visitor. For a lunchtime dish you could make one large tart and serve it with a crisp salad. Easy to prepare in advance and keep in the fridge until ready to cook.

1 tbsp	olive oil	15 ml
1	small red onion, finely sliced	1
2	cloves garlic, crushed	2
1	13-oz pack frozen puff pastry (or see Quick Flaky Pastry recipe, p. 187)	1
2 tbsps	sun-dried tomato paste	2 tsps
1	8-oz can tuna, water-packed, drained	1
12	cherry tomatoes, cut into quarters	12
18	capers, drained	18
12	black olives	12
	fresh basil leaves to garnish	

Pre-heat the oven to 425F. Heat the olive oil in a small pan and sauté the onion and garlic for about 5 minutes, until soft.

Roll pastry until large enough to allow for six, 6 x 6-inch squares. Cut 3/4-inch strips off sides of each square.

Cut these strips to the same length as the squares, wet one side of each strip and stick strips along edges of squares, overlapping at corners. Place the pastry cases on a baking sheet. Prick the inside of each case with a fork.

Spread the sun-dried tomato paste over the inside of the uncooked pastry cases, taking care not to put anything over the side strips.

Spoon one-sixth of the tuna into each pastry case, cover with 8 quarters of tomatoes, 3 capers and some red onion mix. Top with 2 olives.

Bake for 10–15 minutes, until pastry has risen and is golden. Serve hot or warm, garnished with basil leaves.

PER SERVING	
Calories	430
% Calories from fat	56
Fat (g)	27.1
Saturated fat (g)	6.5
Cholesterol (mg)	11.3
Sodium (mg)	489
Protein (g)	14.9
Carbohydrate (g)	32.2
Calcium (mg)	26.5

EXCHANGES	
Milk	0.0
Vegetable	0.0
Fruit	0.0
Bread	2.0
Meat	1.0
Fat	5.0

The filling could be made with other fish such as fresh cooked salmon, cooked smoked haddock, smoked mackerel, smoked salmon, etc.

Smoked Salmon Roulade with Smoked Trout Mousse

Serves 8

This recipe uses mayonnaise and smoked fish to produce a deliciously creamy mousse rolled up in smoked salmon. The end result is extremely impressive and suitable for any occasion, whether it be a summer lunch with salad and French bread or an extremely eye-catching starter. The roulade can be made well in advance and will last for several days in the fridge.

6 oz	smoked salmon, in thin slices	170 g
1	package (¼ oz) gelatin	1
½ cup	soy milk	120 ml
½ cup	low-fat mayonnaise	110 ml
1	smoked trout (weight when skinned and boned about 6 oz)	1
3 tbsps	lemon juice	45 ml
	freshly ground mace	
	sprig fresh dill	
	freshly ground pepper	
	lemon wedges and watercress to garnish	

You will need a rectangular platter about 5 inches by 9 inches, covered with plastic wrap, overlapping the edges. Lay out thin layers of the smoked salmon evenly over the plastic wrap.

Next, soak the gelatin in a bowl of cold water until softened (about 5 minutes). Place the soy milk, mayonnaise and smoked trout in the blender and process quickly until almost smooth.

Heat the lemon juice in a small pan and when hot, remove the pan from the heat and add the gelatin, stirring well until melted. Pour the melted gelatin into the blender with the smoked trout mixture. Process again fairly briefly until thoroughly dispersed.

Mix in ground mace, dill and pepper (you should not need salt because of the saltiness of smoked fish). Spread evenly over the smoked salmon, and chill until set. When the mousse is set, using the plastic wrap, lift the salmon along the long edge of the platter and roll it over and over, pulling away the plastic wrap as it rolls. Secure firmly in place by wrapping the roll in plastic wrap (it should resemble a fat sausage) and chill. To serve, unwrap the roulade and slice it with a sharp knife.

Garnish with lemon wedges and watercress. Serve with hot bread or toast.

PER SERVING	
Calories	114
% Calories from fat	52
Fat (g)	6.7
Saturated fat (g)	1.1
Cholesterol (mg)	12
Sodium (mg)	310
Protein (g)	11.1
Carbohydrate (g)	3
Calcium (mg)	18.1

EXCHANGES	
Milk	0.0
Vegetable	0.0
Fruit	0.0
Bread	0.0
Meat	2.0
Fat	0.0

This dish could also be made with shrimp (freshly shelled even better).

The smaller the squid, the more tender it should be. Take care not to overcook squid, as it becomes tough and rubbery.

Squid with Chilies and Tomatoes

Serves 6 as starter

There was a time when squid was generally only available in an unprepared way, which meant lots of inky mess and strange things to be pulled out of the squid. Not a job for the squeamish cook! Nowadays, it is usually available ready prepared from most fish markets and supermarkets. Squid is quite economical, and the combination of tomatoes and chili peppers makes for an exceptional dish. Serve this with hot Italian bread.

2 tbsps	olive oil (or use the oil from the drained sun-dried tomatoes)	30 ml
2	green onions, finely chopped	2
1	large red chili pepper, de-seeded and finely chopped	1
2	tomatoes, finely chopped	2
1 tbsp	tomato purée	1 tbsp
8	sun-dried tomatoes, oil packed, finely chopped	8
1 tbsp	chopped parsley	1 tbsp
1 tbsp	chopped fresh oregano (could use 1 teaspoon dried)	1 tbsp
1 lb	fresh prepared squid, cut into rings	450 g
	salt and freshly ground pepper	

Heat 1 tablespoon of the oil in a large wok or frying pan until medium hot. Add the green onions, chilies, tomatoes, tomato purée and sun-dried tomatoes and stir quickly for 4 minutes.

Stir the parsley and oregano into the sauce and pour out into a separate dish.

Wash out the wok or pan and add remaining oil. When very hot, add the squid. Toss the squid in the pan quickly for 30 seconds.

Pour in the tomato sauce and mix well with the squid. Season with salt and freshly ground pepper.

Serve hot.

PER SERVING

Calories	133
% Calories from fat	42
Fat (g)	6.3
Saturated fat (g)	1
Cholesterol (mg)	176.1
Sodium (mg)	53.4
Protein (g)	12.7
Carbohydrate (g)	6.6
Calcium (mg)	37.4

EXCHANGES

Milk	0.0
Vegetable	1.0
Fruit	0.0
Bread	0.0
Meat	2.0
Fat	0.0

Chinese-Style Crispy Pork Strips

Serves 8 as starter

These are very easy and very tasty. Try barbecuing instead of broiling for a fabulous dish.

For the Pork Strips

1½ lb	pork loin	675 g
2 tsps	Chinese 5 spice powder	2 tsps
1	red chili pepper, deseeded and chopped	1
2	cloves garlic, peeled and crushed	2
1 inch	piece ginger, finely chopped	2½ cm
	pinch salt	
1 cup	water	240 ml

For the Sauce

2 tbsps	soy sauce	30 ml
1 tbsp	dry sherry	15 ml
1 tbsp	dark brown sugar	25 g
1 tsp	cornstarch	1 tsp

Pre-heat the oven to 350F. Using a sharp knife, cut the meat into about 8 strips.

Lay the pork strips in a large baking dish and cover with the Chinese 5 spice, chili, crushed garlic and chopped ginger and salt.

Pour the water into the dish, cover with aluminum foil and bake for about 1 hour.

Pour off the remaining juice into a small saucepan. Skim off any excess pork fat that may be floating at the top and discard. Place the pork strips on a suitable pan for grilling.

Into the pork juice, stir the soy sauce, sherry and dark brown sugar. Bring to a boil and cook for about 1 minute.

Mix the cornstarch with 1 tbsp water until smooth, and add to the sauce, stirring well. Bring the sauce to a boil and stir until the sauce begins to thicken (if it is too thick add dash of water).

Heat the broiler. Spoon a little of the sauce over the pork strips and broil for about 3 minutes on each side until the strips become crisp.

Heat the sauce and serve with the pork strips.

PER SERVING	
Calories	138
% Calories from fat	31
Fat (g)	4.6
Saturated fat (g)	1.6
Cholesterol (mg)	49.9
Sodium (mg)	303
Protein (g)	18.7
Carbohydrate (g)	3.7
Calcium (mg)	23.8

EXCHANGES	
Milk	0.0
Vegetable	0.0
Fruit	0.0
Bread	0.0
Meat	2.0
Fat	0.0

The longer you marinate the kebabs, the more flavor the chicken will have.

If you are using wooden skewers, soak them in water first to stop them from charring.

Marinated Lime and Sesame Chicken Sticks

Serves 6 as starter

These chicken sticks are quick and easy to prepare and have a delicate Thai flavor. Served simply with a wedge of lime, they provide a nutritious low-fat starter. However, if you want more of a special dish, serve with my hot Peanut and Coconut Chili Sauce.

2	boneless chicken breasts (about 1 lb)	2
2	limes	2
1 tsp	sweet paprika	1 tsp
1 tbsp	sesame oil	15 ml
2	cloves garlic, crushed	2
6	wooden skewers	6
1	red bell pepper, de-seeded and cut into cubes	1
1 tbsp	sesame seeds	1 tbsp
	arugula leaves or salad to garnish	

Remove the skin of the chicken breasts and cut each breast into about 12 cubes.

In a bowl, mix the cubed chicken with the zest and juice of one lime, paprika, sesame oil and garlic. Leave for several hours to marinate in the fridge. Pre-heat broiler.

Spike the cubed chicken onto the skewers alternating with the red pepper.

Lay the chicken sticks under the hot broiler for about 15 minutes, turning from time to time to ensure even cooking. Halfway through the cooking, drizzle over any remaining sesame and lime marinade.

Sprinkle the chicken sticks all over with the sesame seeds. Serve each chicken stick on a small warm plate and drizzle over any cooking juices.

Garnish with some arugula leaves and a wedge of lime.

PER SERVING	
Calories	129
% Calories from fat	28
Fat (g)	4
Saturated fat (g)	0.7
Cholesterol (mg)	45.6
Sodium (mg)	42
Protein (g)	18.9
Carbohydrate (g)	4.5
Calcium (mg)	34.6

EXCHANGES	
Milk	0.0
Vegetable	0.0
Fruit	0.0
Bread	0.0
Meat	2.0
Fat	0.0

This salad may also be made with smoked chicken breast.

Smoked Duck Salad with Spiced Walnuts

Serves 6 as starter

This starter is a real treat and easy to prepare in advance, without spooning over the dressing. The smoked duck tastes wonderful with the sweet and sour flavor of the onion marmalade and the spiciness of the walnuts.

Smoked duck is quite a luxury ingredient and fairly expensive, but cut thinly it goes quite a long way. You should find it in your local delicatessen or buy it mail order from a smokery.

2	bunches crisp romaine lettuce leaves	2
¹/₂ recipe	Spiced Walnuts (see page 125)	¹/₂ recipe
1	smoked duck breast, skin and fat removed (about 8 oz)	1
³/₈ cup	Tarragon French Dressing (see page 139)	90 ml
4 tbsps	Onion Marmalade (see page 124)	100 g

Wash and dry the lettuce, and break it into pieces. Distribute the lettuce onto six individual plates. Sprinkle the spiced walnuts over the lettuce.

Next, slice the smoked duck into thin strips. Lay thin slices of the smoked duck over the top of each salad.

Drizzle a couple of spoonfuls of dressing over each plate.

Finally, dollop a teaspoon of the onion marmalade onto the sliced duck.

Serve with crisp warm French bread.

PER SERVING	
Calories	321
% Calories from fat	76
Fat (g)	27.9
Saturated fat (g)	3.9
Cholesterol (mg)	33.6
Sodium (mg)	226
Protein (g)	13
Carbohydrate (g)	6.7
Calcium (mg)	50.2

EXCHANGES	
Milk	0.0
Vegetable	0.0
Fruit	0.0
Bread	0.0
Meat	2.0
Fat	5.0

Vary the nuts according to what you have in your cupboard. For a much creamier texture, increase the quantity of peanut butter. Also, almond butter is a nice substitute for peanut butter.

Mushroom and Nut Pâté

Serves 10

This tasty vegetarian pâté is made with a mixture of lentils and nuts. The addition of peanut butter enables the pâté to become rich and creamy in texture. It will keep well up to about 8 days in the fridge and makes a quick and nutritious snack. Try spreading it on hot toast or with grated carrot in a crispy sandwich.

3/4 cup	uncooked red lentils (6 oz)	170 g
3 cups	water for cooking lentils	700 ml
1 tbsp	olive oil	1 tbsp
1	large or 2 medium onions, finely chopped	1
2	cloves garlic, crushed	2
3 cups	button mushrooms, wiped and very finely chopped (7 oz)	200 g
1 tsp	vegan bouillon powder	1 tsp
1 tsp	ground cumin	1 tsp
1/2 tsp	ground turmeric	1/2 tsp
1 tsp	ground cilantro	1 tsp
1/2 tsp	chili powder	1/2 tsp
1 tsp	Dijon mustard	1 tsp
3 tbsps	crunchy peanut butter	3 tbsps
	juice of 1/2 lemon	
3/4 cup	ground, roasted hazelnuts (2 1/2 oz)	3/4 cup
1 tbsp	chopped fresh cilantro (save a few leaves for garnish)	1 tbsp
	salt and freshly ground pepper	

PER SERVING	
Calories	217
% Calories from fat	56
Fat (g)	14.2
Saturated fat (g)	1.5
Cholesterol (mg)	0
Sodium (mg)	132
Protein (g)	9.5
Carbohydrate (g)	15.9
Calcium (mg)	37.4
EXCHANGES	
Milk	0.0
Vegetable	0.0
Fruit	0.0
Bread	1.0
Meat	1.0
Fat	2.0

Rinse the lentils in a sieve under cold water. Put the lentils in a large saucepan with the water and bring to a boil. Skim off any scum that forms.

Boil gently for 10–15 minutes until soft, but not completely mushy. Strain through a sieve and leave to dry.

Next, heat a large frying pan with the oil, add the onion and garlic and cook for about 5 minutes until beginning to soften.

Mix in the mushrooms, stir well and cook for several minutes. Add bouillon powder and spices and sauté for about 4 minutes until mixture dries out. Transfer to a large bowl. Add the cooked lentils, mustard, peanut butter, lemon juice, roasted nuts, cilantro and seasonings. Refrigerate for at least 1 hour. Serve, smoothed into individual ramekins, each garnished with a cilantro leaf.

Omit anchovies for a vegan alternative. Try using different toppings, such as grilled eggplant, bell peppers, asparagus or marinated artichoke hearts. For the meat eater, thin slices of ham or bacon would be delicious with the tomatoes.

Important note—try to use fresh young garlic, as some older garlic becomes bitter and unpleasant in taste.

Roasted Cherry Tomato Bruschetta

Serves 4

Bruschetta are little Italian toasts, an excellent way of using up any leftover stale French or Italian bread. The combination of flavors and the olive oil on crisp toasts make a delicious Mediterranean-style dish also suitable for a light summer lunch, especially when you have a glut of small tomatoes.

Do not be alarmed by the amount of garlic used, as the cooking process takes away the strong taste associated with raw garlic. Boiling the garlic beforehand allows easy peeling and begins to cook it slightly.

8	cloves garlic, unpeeled	8
1	medium red onion, cut in half and sliced	1
1/4 cup	olive oil	60 ml
2 tbsps	capers, rinsed	2 tbsps
1	2-oz can anchovy fillets in oil, drained	1
24	cherry tomatoes	24
	freshly ground pepper	
1 tbsp	balsamic vinegar	15 ml
1	demi-baguette French bread (about 8 inches)	1
2 tbsps	vegan pesto (found in health food shops; alternatively you can use sun-dried tomato paste)	2 tbsps
	garnish with fresh basil leaves	

PER SERVING	
Calories	366
% Calories from fat	45
Fat (g)	18.5
Saturated fat (g)	2.9
Cholesterol (mg)	13.9
Sodium (mg)	1063
Protein (g)	11.4
Carbohydrate (g)	39.5
Calcium (mg)	115.1

EXCHANGES	
Milk	0.0
Vegetable	2.0
Fruit	0.0
Bread	2.0
Meat	0.0
Fat	4.0

Pre-heat the oven to 400F. Put garlic cloves in small pan of cold water, bring to boil and cook for 2–3 minutes; drain and peel.

In a large oven dish, roast the red onion and garlic cloves mixed with 1/8 cup of the olive oil in the oven for about 10 minutes. Remove from the oven and stir in the capers, halved anchovy fillets, cherry tomatoes and freshly ground pepper. Return to the oven and roast for a further 15 minutes. Stir in the balsamic vinegar.

Meanwhile, slice the bread into about 8 slices and place them on a baking sheet. Drizzle with the remaining olive oil and some more pepper. Bake for about 5 minutes, turn the bread slices over and repeat for several minutes until golden and crisp.

Spread pesto onto the crisp bruschettas and spoon over the hot tomato mix and any remaining roasting juices. Garnish with fresh basil leaves.

If it is easier, use about 6 oz frozen, defrosted spinach. Squeeze out excess water and add to onions while still frying. Also delicious with chopped sun-dried tomatoes added to the filling. If you are unable to buy pine nuts, you could use flaked almonds for an interesting texture and flavor.

Crispy Spinach and Pine Nut Filo Parcels

Serves 8 (1 parcel per serving)

These are a great way to start a meal. You can serve them with the Sun-Dried Tomato, Basil and Garlic Dressing on page 143. Or serve as a light meal with Tomato and Pimiento Coulis on page 121.

If made slightly smaller by cutting the sheets into 3, they are a great idea for canapés. The addition of mustard gives them more of a savory flavor.

6–7 cups	fresh spinach leaves (about 10 oz)	280 g
1	medium onion, finely chopped	1
2	cloves garlic, crushed	2
1 tbsp	olive oil	15 ml
2/3 cup	soy cream cheese	150 g
1 tbsp	Dijon mustard	1 tbsp
2 tbsps	pine nuts	2 tbsps
	good pinch of grated nutmeg	
	salt and freshly ground pepper	
4	sheets of filo pastry, thawed if frozen	4
1 1/2 tbsps	vegan margarine, melted	37 g

Pre-heat the oven to 400F. Wash and trim stalks from the spinach. Put the spinach leaves into a large saucepan, covered, over a medium heat and cook for approximately 5 minutes.

Drain, rinse under cold water and press down in a sieve to drain off any excess water. Chop the spinach once it is drained of excess water.

In a frying pan, gently cook the onion and garlic in the olive oil for about 8 minutes or until soft and beginning to caramelize. Mix in the chopped spinach, cream cheese, mustard, pine nuts and seasonings.

Keep the filo pastry under a damp tea cloth until required.

Taking one sheet at a time, cut in half lengthways and brush with melted margarine.

Spoon an eighth of the filling onto one end of the pastry strip. Fold diagonally and again until you reach the end, having made a triangular parcel.

Place parcels on an oiled baking sheet. Bake for 15–20 minutes until crisp and golden brown. Serve hot.

PER SERVING	
Calories	140
% Calories from fat	70
Fat (g)	10.9
Saturated fat (g)	2.3
Cholesterol (mg)	0
Sodium (mg)	247
Protein (g)	3.1
Carbohydrate (g)	7.5
Calcium (mg)	34.2

EXCHANGES	
Milk	0.0
Vegetable	0.0
Fruit	0.0
Bread	0.5
Meat	0.0
Fat	2.0

You could use warm pita bread instead of tortillas.

Hummus, Chili and Crisp Vegetable Wrap

Serves 4 (1 wrap per serving)

This is an ideal vegan snack that can be taken to work and eaten cold or warmed up slightly in the oven or microwave.

4	flour tortillas, about 8 inch diameter	4
1/4 cup	hummus (shop bought or homemade)	1/4 cup
4 tsps	sweet chili sauce (or hot chili sauce if desired)	4 tsps
1 cup	finely shredded red or green cabbage	110 g
2	medium carrots, peeled and grated	2
	freshly ground pepper	

Warm the tortillas according to manufacturer's instructions. Spread 1 tablespoon hummus, followed by 1 teaspoon of chili sauce on each tortilla. Sprinkle over cabbage, carrot and pepper. Roll up each tortilla into a roll and serve.

VEGAN

PER SERVING	
Calories	157
% Calories from fat	21
Fat (g)	3.7
Saturated fat (g)	0.8
Cholesterol (mg)	0
Sodium (mg)	364
Protein (g)	4.2
Carbohydrate (g)	27.3
Calcium (mg)	69.9
EXCHANGES	
Milk	0.0
Vegetable	0.0
Fruit	0.0
Bread	2.0
Meat	0.0
Fat	0.5

Bacon, Tomato and Watercress Wrap

Serves 4 (1 wrap per serving)

This wrap has a hot filling and is best assembled just before serving. The roasted tomatoes prevent the filling from becoming dry and make a mouth-watering combination with the bacon and watercress.

6	slices smoked or unsmoked bacon	6
4	medium tomatoes, quartered	4
2	green onions, chopped	2
	drizzle of olive oil	
2 tsps	balsamic vinegar	10 ml
4	flour tortillas, about 8 inch diameter	4
1 tbsp	sun-dried tomato paste	1 tbsp
1	small bunch of watercress	1
	freshly ground pepper	

Pre-heat the oven to 400F. In a large baking dish, arrange the bacon at one end. At other end place the quartered tomatoes, sprinkled with green onions.

Drizzle over a little olive oil and the balsamic vinegar. Grind on some black pepper.

Roast in the oven for 10 minutes, until the tomatoes are soft and the bacon is cooked.

Warm tortillas slightly according to manufacturer's instructions. Spread a little sun-dried tomato paste over each tortilla.

Spoon tomato and onion mixture onto each tortilla and spread around.

Sprinkle the roughly chopped bacon and watercress over the tomatoes.

Roll up each tortilla and serve immediately.

PER SERVING

Calories	207
% Calories from fat	37
Fat (g)	8.6
Saturated fat (g)	2.7
Cholesterol (mg)	10.2
Sodium (mg)	393
Protein (g)	8
Carbohydrate (g)	25.4
Calcium (mg)	64.6

EXCHANGES

Milk	0.0
Vegetable	0.0
Fruit	0.0
Bread	2.0
Meat	0.0
Fat	1.5

Light Meals and Lunches

Caribbean-Style Spare Ribs

Moroccan Lamb Burgers

Smoked Ham and Lentil Pie

Baked Eggs in Pancetta and Mushroom Tartlets

*Risotto of Artichoke Hearts and
Mushrooms Topped with Parma Ham*

Caramelized Onion, Bacon and Red Lentil Quiche

Spaghetti, Carbonara Style

*Sautéed Chicken Livers in Wine and
Sage Sauce on Garlic Bread Croutons*

Spicy Chicken Quesadillas

Grilled Fresh Tuna on Potato Niçoise

Smoked Salmon and Spinach Quiche

Potato Pancakes

Eggplant and Red Lentil Loaf

Baked Stuffed Mushrooms

Chick Peas with Tomatoes and Cilantro

Curried Spinach and Eggs

Potato, Bean and Corn Frittata

Sweet Potato and Chick Pea Cakes

Caribbean-Style Spare Ribs

Serves 8

Pork ribs are an affordable cut of meat. These deliciously messy ribs make an ideal meal for summer barbecues and should be popular with all the family.

1	onion, peeled and roughly chopped	1
2	small or 1 large red chili peppers, de-seeded and quartered	2
3	garlic cloves	3
1 tsp	ground allspice	1 tsp
1/2 tsp	ground cinnamon	1/2 tsp
1 inch	piece of fresh gingerroot, peeled and roughly chopped	2.5 cm
	handful fresh thyme sprigs, leaves removed or 1 teaspoon dried	
1/4 tsp	ground black pepper	1/4 tsp
	juice and grated zest of 1 lime	
5 tbsps	cider vinegar or white wine vinegar	75 ml
1/2 cup	dark soy sauce	120 ml
2 tbsps	dark superfine sugar	50 g
3 tbsps	peanut or sunflower oil	45 ml
4 lb	pork ribs	1.8 kg

Place the onion, chilies, garlic, allspice, cinnamon, ginger, thyme and black pepper in food processor and purée for about 30 seconds until well blended.

Add the lime juice and zest, vinegar, soy sauce, sugar and oil and process again until it becomes a purée consistency.

Lay the pork ribs in a large glass or ceramic (non-metallic) baking dish. Pour the marinade over the ribs.

Marinate in the fridge for 4–24 hours, basting occasionally.

Cook on a barbecue grill, basting occasionally with marinade; cook the remaining sauce in a pan and serve with the ribs.

Alternatively, grill under a low to medium pre-heated broiler for about 25–30 minutes turning occasionally and brushing with marinade, until tender inside but beginning to char on the edges.

PER SERVING	
Calories	730
% Calories from fat	72
Fat (g)	56.4
Saturated fat (g)	20.1
Cholesterol (mg)	115.2
Sodium (mg)	1106
Protein (g)	40.7
Carbohydrate (g)	8.6
Calcium (mg)	31.5

EXCHANGES	
Milk	0.0
Vegetable	0.0
Fruit	0.0
Bread	0.5
Meat	6.0
Fat	9.0

Add fresh chili for a hot and fiery touch. Moroccan dishes sometimes use prunes—try them instead of the apricots for a different taste.

Moroccan Lamb Burgers

Serves 4

Moroccan dishes are becoming increasingly popular. The balance of fruit and spices makes these burgers an interesting addition to a barbecue or a light lunch.

The stickiness of the chopped apricots holds the burger together surprisingly well, and they also add a sweetness that may appeal to children. Serve with Harissa Dressing (see page 141) and Spiced Rice (see page 109).

1	small onion, peeled and quartered	1
1 inch	piece fresh gingerroot, peeled and chopped	2.5 cm
2	cloves garlic	2
1	small bunch cilantro, washed	1
1 tsp	ground cinnamon	1 tsp
1 1/2 tsps	ground cilantro	1 1/2 tsps
1 1/2 tsps	ground cumin	1 1/2 tsps
1/2 cup	dried apricots, finely chopped	1/2 cup
1 lb	lean ground lamb	450 g
	salt and freshly ground pepper	

Place the onion, ginger, garlic and cilantro in a food processor and finely chop.

Add the spices, apricots, lamb and salt and pepper, and pulse briefly, keeping the mixture chunky.

Shape into four burgers; refrigerate until required.

Heat a large non-stick frying pan. Cook the burgers for about 5 minutes on either side, and press down with a spatula occasionally to cook through.

Alternatively, cook on a barbecue grill or under a hot broiler on an oiled baking sheet.

Burgers should be dark golden brown and just cooked through.

PER SERVING	
Calories	337
% Calories from fat	57
Fat (g)	21.6
Saturated fat (g)	9.1
Cholesterol (mg)	77.4
Sodium (mg)	60
Protein (g)	20.2
Carbohydrate (g)	15.8
Calcium (mg)	49.6
EXCHANGES	
Milk	0.0
Vegetable	0.0
Fruit	1.0
Bread	0.0
Meat	3.0
Fat	2.0

For a vegan (dairy- and egg-free vegetarian) dish, substitute chopped mushrooms for the ham and saute with the onion.

Smoked Ham and Lentil Pie

Serves 4

This is an inexpensive and hearty pie. The nutty lentils mixed with the ham are particularly tasty with the wholegrain mustard mashed potato topping. Try serving this with lightly steamed green vegetables or a crisp salad.

³/₄ cup	brown lentils (6 oz)	170 g
1 tbsp	olive oil or sunflower oil	15 ml
1	medium onion, finely chopped	1
2	cloves garlic, crushed	2
³/₄ lb	ham hock, weight of meat off the bone and diced (smoked or unsmoked)	337 g
1	14-oz can chopped tomatoes	1
1 tbsp	tomato purée	1 tbsp
	sprig of fresh thyme	
	freshly ground pepper	
1 recipe	Wholegrain Mustard Mashed Potatoes (see page 103)	1 recipe

Pre-heat the oven to 400F. Rinse the lentils. Cover with plenty of cold water in a large saucepan, bring to a boil, cover and simmer gently for about 20–25 minutes until the lentils are soft. Drain well.

In a large saucepan, heat the oil and cook the onion and garlic for about 5 minutes until soft.

Stir in the diced ham and cook for a further 5 minutes.

Tip in the chopped tomatoes and tomato purée, and mix well. Cover the pan and simmer for about 15 minutes. Season with thyme and ground pepper.

You will probably not need salt, as the ham will make the dish salty enough.

Pour into a large baking dish. Cover with wholegrain mustard mashed potatoes and smooth down with a fork.

Put into the hot oven and cook for about 25 minutes until golden, broiling the top if necessary to make a crisp golden topping before serving.

PER SERVING	
Calories	544
% Calories from fat	25
Fat (g)	15
Saturated fat (g)	3.5
Cholesterol (mg)	49.3
Sodium (mg)	1537
Protein (g)	38.6
Carbohydrate (g)	65.3
Calcium (mg)	78.7
EXCHANGES	
Milk	0.0
Vegetable	1.0
Fruit	0.0
Bread	4.0
Meat	3.0
Fat	1.0

For a vegetarian alternative, substitute the pancetta with freshly steamed, drained and chopped spinach well seasoned with freshly ground nutmeg.

Baked Eggs in Pancetta and Mushroom Tartlets

Serves 6

These make a wonderful light meal. The tartlets can be prepared in advance and up to the stage before the egg is added. The baked egg in the middle gives the tartlet a lovely richness, especially if the yolk remains slightly runny. Serve with a dressed salad.

1 recipe	Shortcrust Pastry (see recipe on page 187 or use a suitable bought pastry)	1 recipe
1	large onion, finely chopped	1
2	cloves garlic, crushed	2
1 tbsp	vegetable oil	15 ml
2 cups	mushrooms, finely chopped (6 oz)	170 g
5–6 slices	pancetta (or smoked back bacon), chopped (about 4 oz)	112 g
1 tbsp	chopped parsley (or French tarragon if available)	1 tbsp
	salt and freshly ground pepper	
6	eggs (free range if possible)	6

You will also need 6 quiche pans with 4 inch base diameter, 1/2 inch deep, and a 51/2-inch-diameter round cookie cutter

Pre-heat the oven to 350F. Roll out the pastry on a floured surface to a thickness of about 1/8 inch and large enough to cut out six 51/2-inch rounds.

Grease the pans and line each with the pastry; prick the base with a fork. Allow pastry cases to relax in the fridge for about 30 minutes.

Then place the pans on a solid baking sheet in the hot oven for about 10–15 minutes until golden. Remove from oven. Sauté the chopped onion and garlic in the oil for about 5 minutes until soft.

Add the mushrooms, and cook for several minutes; if the mixture becomes wet, increase temperature and cook out the liquid. Remove from heat and add pancetta, parsley and seasonings.

Spoon this mushroom mixture into the tartlet cases, making a well in the center. Then break an egg into a small cup, and tip this into center of tartlet. Repeat with remaining tartlets.

Return to oven for 12–15 minutes or until just set and yolks are still soft and creamy. Remove from the pans and serve immediately, as the eggs will continue cooking.

PER SERVING	
Calories	287
% Calories from fat	57
Fat (g)	18.2
Saturated fat (g)	5.2
Cholesterol (mg)	221
Sodium (mg)	194
Protein (g)	11
Carbohydrate (g)	19.5
Calcium (mg)	37.2

EXCHANGES	
Milk	0.0
Vegetable	1.0
Fruit	0.0
Bread	1.0
Meat	1.0
Fat	3.0

Omit ham for vegans and use a good vegetable stock. Alternatively, try using smoked salmon instead of ham.

If you have fresh artichokes, you may wish to cook these and remove the hearts, which is quite a time-consuming job, but well worth it.

Risotto of Artichoke Hearts and Mushrooms Topped with Parma Ham

Serves 4

Many people are now realizing that risottos are actually quite simple to make and can be tackled at home. The combination of artichokes, mushrooms and Parma ham makes this creamy risotto extremely appetizing. Serve with a crisp salad.

2 tbsps	olive oil	30 ml
1¼ cups	button mushrooms, wiped and sliced (about 8 oz)	225 g
8	marinated artichoke hearts, drained and quartered	8
1	red onion, finely chopped	1
2	cloves garlic, crushed	2
1 cup	(scant) Arborio rice (7 oz)	196 g
5 tbsps	dry white wine	75 ml
2¾ cups	chicken stock, heated	660 ml
1 tbsp	soy cream	15 ml
	salt and freshly ground pepper	
4 oz	thinly sliced Parma ham, cut in thin strips	112 g
	whole chives cut in half to garnish	

Heat frying pan with 1 tablespoon olive oil, and sauté the sliced mushrooms. After about 4 minutes add the artichoke hearts; cook briefly, then tip into a bowl and set aside.

Meanwhile, heat remaining oil in a large saucepan, and sauté the red onion and garlic for about 5 minutes until soft.

Add the rice, remove from heat and stir until rice is coated. Return the pan to the heat, add all the wine and then 2 ladlefuls of stock. Simmer, stirring constantly until the rice has absorbed nearly all the liquid; add more stock and repeat.

After 20–25 minutes, nearly all the stock will have been absorbed by the rice, and each grain will have a creamy coating but remain al dente.

Add the artichokes and mushrooms to the rice, and heat through. Just before serving, add the soy cream and seasonings.

Spoon onto four warm plates garnished with strips of Parma ham and chives.

PER SERVING	
Calories	384
% Calories from fat	37
Fat (g)	15.5
Saturated fat (g)	2.7
Cholesterol (mg)	33.6
Sodium (mg)	695
Protein (g)	15.2
Carbohydrate (g)	42.2
Calcium (mg)	13.2

EXCHANGES	
Milk	0.0
Vegetable	2.0
Fruit	0.0
Bread	2.0
Meat	1.0
Fat	3.0

Omit bacon for a vegetarian version. The whole wheat pastry in this recipe does not require much pre-cooking.

Caramelized Onion, Bacon and Red Lentil Quiche

Serves 6

This is not your typical creamy quiche filling, although the red lentils break down enough to give it a smooth, wholesome texture, which is very nutritious, and the mustard gives added flavor. Serve warm or cold with a crisp salad.

1 recipe	Whole Wheat Pastry (see page 188)	1 recipe
½ cup	dried red lentils (3 oz)	84 g
2	medium to large onions, peeled and sliced in half rings	2
1 tbsp	olive oil	15 ml
5–6 slices	unsmoked or smoked back bacon, rind removed, diced (about 4 oz)	112 g
1 tsp	vegan bouillon powder	1 tsp
1 cup	(scant) soy milk	200 ml
1 tbsp	Dijon mustard	1 tbsp
	2 eggs plus 2 egg whites, beaten together	
	salt and freshly ground pepper	
1 tbsp	chopped parsley	1 tbsp
1	sprig of fresh thyme	1

Pre-heat the oven to 350F. Lightly grease a 9-inch flan or quiche dish (a deeper dish is preferable, as this has quite a substantial amount of filling).

Roll out the pastry and line the baking dish, easing any overlapping pastry back into the sides. Prick the base with a fork, and bake in the oven for 5 minutes to set the pastry.

Meanwhile, rinse the lentils and place in a small pan covered with plenty of water. Bring to a boil, then simmer for 8–10 minutes until almost cooked but not mushy; drain well.

In a large frying pan, sauté the onions with the olive oil over medium heat for about 10 minutes, stirring well. Remove from heat when soft and beginning to caramelize.

Add the bacon to the onions, and cook over medium heat for a further 4 minutes until just cooked. Stir in the lentils. Set aside.

In a large bowl, blend the bouillon powder with 2 tablespoons of boiling water, add the soy milk, mustard and eggs and season with salt and freshly ground pepper. Mix well, then finally stir in the chopped parsley and thyme leaves.

Spoon the onion and lentil mixture into the half-cooked pastry case. Carefully pour the egg mixture into the pastry case so that all the filling is well covered. Return to oven and cook for about 35 minutes until risen, firm and golden.

PER SERVING	
Calories	390
% Calories from fat	55
Fat (g)	23.2
Saturated fat (g)	6
Cholesterol (mg)	78.6
Sodium (mg)	600
Protein (g)	13.7
Carbohydrate (g)	29.3
Calcium (mg)	131.8

EXCHANGES	
Milk	0.0
Vegetable	0.0
Fruit	0.0
Bread	2.0
Meat	1.0
Fat	4.0

For a vegetarian dish, omit bacon. You could add walnuts for a more nutritious meal.

For a vegan dish, omit both bacon and egg.

Spaghetti, Carbonara Style

Serves 4

The idea of adding hummus to hot spaghetti may seem a bit strange. The result, however, is surprisingly delicious and creamy, with a slightly grainy texture not too dissimilar to Parmesan. Serve an arugula or lettuce salad with this pasta dish.

1 tbsp	olive oil	15 ml
1	medium onion, peeled and finely chopped	1
2	cloves garlic, crushed	2
5–6 slices	smoked bacon, diced (about 4 oz)	112 g
2/3 cup	button mushrooms, wiped and sliced (about 4 oz)	112 g
12 oz	dried spaghetti or tagliatelle	340 g
1/2 cup	hummus (the bought variety is excellent for this dish)	1/2 cup
1 tbsp	mild Dijon mustard	1 tbsp
2	egg yolks	2
2 tbsps	finely chopped parsley	2 tbsps
	salt and freshly ground pepper	

Heat the oil in a saucepan, add onions and garlic and sauté gently for 5 minutes, stirring continuously.

Next, add the diced bacon and, stirring well, cook for 2 minutes; then add the mushrooms and cook for a further 4 minutes on a slightly higher heat.

Set aside while you cook pasta. Don't worry if the mushrooms become slightly wet, as the pasta will absorb any liquid.

Cook the pasta in boiling salted water for 8–10 minutes or until al dente (tender but still firm to the bite). Drain well.

Immediately toss the pasta with the mushroom and bacon mixture, return to low heat, add hummus, mustard, egg yolks and half the parsley and season well. Stir the pasta well over a low heat for several minutes to cook the yolks, although not too hot or you will curdle the yolks.

To serve: tip on to warm plates and sprinkle over the remaining parsley.

PER SERVING	
Calories	506
% Calories from fat	27
Fat (g)	14.9
Saturated fat (g)	3.6
Cholesterol (mg)	114.8
Sodium (mg)	333
Protein (g)	17.6
Carbohydrate (g)	73.5
Calcium (mg)	54.7

EXCHANGES	
Milk	0.0
Vegetable	3.0
Fruit	0.0
Bread	4.0
Meat	0.0
Fat	3.0

Try this dish with mushrooms for a delicious vegan alternative. It can also be served as a starter for 8 with one crouton each.

Sautéed Chicken Livers in Wine and Sage Sauce on Garlic Bread Croutons

Serves 4

Chicken livers are extremely economical and nutritious. They can usually be bought in tubs frozen from the butcher. This recipe incorporates them in a fairly sophisticated dish. The croutons add to the texture and appearance of the dish.

For the croutons

8	slices thick-cut white bread	8
4	cloves garlic, crushed to a smooth paste	4
2 tbsps	olive oil	30 ml

For the chicken livers

1 lb	chicken livers, defrosted if frozen	450 g
1 tbsp	olive oil	15 ml
2	small shallots, finely chopped	2
12	fresh sage leaves	12
1/4 cup	dry white wine	60 ml
1/4 cup	fat-free chicken stock or vegetable stock	60 ml
1/4 cup	soy cream	60 ml
	salt and freshly ground black pepper	
	chopped parsley to garnish	

Pre-heat the oven to 375F. Using a large round cutter, or a cup, cut out 8 discs from the slices of bread. You can use the remainder for breadcrumbs.

Lay the bread on a large baking sheet and spread each bread disc with garlic, coating them well.

Drizzle the olive oil over the garlic bread discs and bake them in the oven for 10–15 minutes, until golden and crisp. Keep warm when cooked.

Meanwhile, prepare the chicken livers. Examine livers carefully for green spots, and cut these away and remove any bits of fat.

Rinse the livers in cold water, then gently pat dry with paper towels.

Next, heat the oil in a large frying pan and sauté the shallots for about 4 minutes.

Turn the heat up high and add the chicken livers and sage leaves.

Cook for about 2 minutes, turning frequently, until the livers lose their raw, red color.

Transfer the chicken livers and sage to a warm plate, using a slotted spoon.

Pour the wine and stock into the hot pan, and simmer for about 1 minute, scraping the pan well to remove cooking residues.

Return the livers to the pan and heat thoroughly.

Lower the heat, stir in the soy cream and season well.

Place a crouton on each of the four plates, and spoon the livers and sauce over each crouton.

Top with another crouton placed at an angle. Sprinkle with chopped parsley and serve immediately.

PER SERVING	
Calories	402
% Calories from fat	40
Fat (g)	17.5
Saturated fat (g)	3.1
Cholesterol (mg)	499.9
Sodium (mg)	382
Protein (g)	25.4
Carbohydrate (g)	31.7
Calcium (mg)	93.6

EXCHANGES	
Milk	0.0
Vegetable	0.0
Fruit	0.0
Bread	2.0
Meat	3.0
Fat	2.0

Spicy Chicken Quesadillas

Serves 4

Mexican food is always extremely popular. It is a fun way of cooking, with lots of diverse and interesting flavors. These quesadillas can be kept in the fridge, rolled and ready to cook, so when your friends arrive there is very little work left to do. What's so good about this dish is that if you are cooking for lots of people, some of whom may eat dairy, you can vary the cheese accordingly.

1 lb	skinned chicken breast	450 g
2 tsps	ground cumin	2 tsps
2	cloves garlic, crushed	2
2 tsps	ground cilantro	2 tsps
1/2 tsp	chili powder	1/2 tsp
2 tbsps	peanut oil	30 ml
8	flour (or corn) tortillas	8
4	green onions, sliced	4
1	red bell pepper, de-seeded and thinly sliced	1
2	jalapeño green chilies, thinly sliced	2
8	slices of soy mozzarella	8

Cut the chicken into thin strips and place in bowl with cumin, garlic, cilantro and chili powder. Mix well, then leave to marinate in the fridge for 2 hours.

Heat half a tablespoon of the oil and fry the chicken strips in batches, until golden and just cooked through.

Soften the tortillas in a microwave or follow manufacturer's instructions.

Mix the green onions, red bell pepper, chilies and chicken in a bowl.

Divide chicken mixture among tortillas, folding and rolling each to enclose filling.

To re-heat, cook in batches seam-sides down in a large, hot frying pan with the remaining oil, turning occasionally until golden.

Cover each quesadilla with a slice of soy mozzarella and place under a hot broiler until the mozzarella just starts to melt. Serve immediately.

Use bought tortillas or follow recipe on page 127 for homemade Flour Tortillas.

If you are unable to get soy mozzarella and want a touch of something resembling sour cream, try spooning onto the tortillas a dollop of Tofu and Almond Cream on page 170.

Serve with Chili Bean Salsa (see page 114) or Roasted Sweetcorn and Lime Salsa (see page 118).

PER SERVING	
Calories	549
% Calories from fat	35
Fat (g)	21
Saturated fat (g)	3.6
Cholesterol (mg)	65.7
Sodium (mg)	756
Protein (g)	44.7
Carbohydrate (g)	42.5
Calcium (mg)	420.6

EXCHANGES	
Milk	0.0
Vegetable	0.0
Fruit	0.0
Bread	3.0
Meat	5.0
Fat	1.0

If fresh tuna is unavailable, or for a picnic, use canned tuna steak, drained and mixed with the potato salad.

Plunging cooked vegetables into cold water helps retain a good green color and prevents further cooking.

Grilled Fresh Tuna on Potato Niçoise

Serves 4

This well-balanced light meal is great for barbecues if you make salad and dressing in advance, then barbecue the fish to order.

Fresh tuna is now readily available in most supermarkets, and being an oily fish, it contains the essential fatty acids.

5–6	small new potatoes (about 8 oz)	225 g
3/4 cup	stringbeans (about 4 oz)	112 g
2 tbsp	capers, drained	2 tbsp
8	sun-dried tomatoes, oil packed, drained and chopped	8
1/4 cup	pitted black olives	1/4 cup
14	cherry tomatoes, washed and halved	14
4	6-oz tuna loin steaks cut about 3/4 inch thick	4
	double recipe of the Sun-Dried Tomato, Basil and Garlic Dressing (see page 143)	
	fresh basil to garnish	

Boil or steam the new potatoes until cooked but not too soft.

Steam the stringbeans, and when cooked but still crisp, refresh by running cold water over them.

Mix potatoes, beans, capers, sun-dried tomatoes, olives and tomatoes in bowl, and refrigerate.

To cook the tuna, lightly oil a non-stick skillet, place over a high heat, and when hot put in tuna steaks for about 1 minute.

When the tuna steaks have changed to a white color two-thirds of the way through, carefully turn the steaks and cook for a few more seconds.

Spoon the potato salad mixture onto 4 plates.

Arrange the tuna on top of the potato salad and drizzle about 2 tablespoons of dressing over the top of each plate; garnish with fresh basil leaves.

PER SERVING	
Calories	406
% Calories from fat	38
Fat (g)	17.2
Saturated fat (g)	2.5
Cholesterol (mg)	75.8
Sodium (mg)	351
Protein (g)	43.5
Carbohydrate (g)	20
Calcium (mg)	70.6
EXCHANGES	
Milk	0.0
Vegetable	1.0
Fruit	0.0
Bread	1.0
Meat	1.0
Fat	2.0

Try making this quiche with smoked haddock for another delicious combination.

Smoked Salmon and Spinach Quiche

Serves 4

Most savory quiches contain cheese; however, the combination of spinach and smoked salmon is so delicious that you forget about the missing cheese completely. Quite often fish markets will have inexpensive salmon offcuts. These are ideal for this quiche, as the salmon is chopped up. This quiche may be served hot, warm or cold with a mixed leaf or tomato salad.

4–5 cups	fresh spinach (5 oz)	140 g
1 recipe	Shortcrust Pastry (see recipe on page 187 or use a suitable bought pastry)	1 recipe
1/2 cup	soy cream cheese	110 g
2/3 cup	soy milk	160 ml
1	large egg plus 1 egg yolk, beaten	1
1 tbsp	Dijon mustard	1 tbsp
	freshly grated nutmeg	
	salt and freshly ground pepper	
1/2 cup	chopped smoked salmon (4 oz)	112 g

Pre-heat the oven to 350F. To prepare the spinach, wash well and either steam for 2 minutes or place in a large covered pan and heat until wilted; refresh by running it under cold water. Squeeze dry and chop.

Roll out the pastry on a floured surface and line a greased 8-inch quiche dish, easing any overlapping pastry back into the sides; prick base with a fork. Bake the pastry case blind, using greaseproof paper and dried beans, for 15 minutes on the center shelf.

Remove from the oven, and take out the paper and beans. Return to the oven for a few more minutes to dry.

Beat the cream cheese with the soy milk until smooth. Add the eggs, mustard, nutmeg and seasonings, stirring well.

Arrange the chopped spinach and the smoked salmon evenly on the pastry base. Pour the egg mixture over the spinach and salmon.

Bake at 350F for 25–30 minutes until the center is set and the filling golden and puffy.

PER SERVING	
Calories	374
% Calories from fat	58
Fat (g)	23.6
Saturated fat (g)	6.4
Cholesterol (mg)	65.7
Sodium (mg)	569
Protein (g)	13
Carbohydrate (g)	25.8
Calcium (mg)	42.7
EXCHANGES	
Milk	0.0
Vegetable	0.0
Fruit	0.0
Bread	2.0
Meat	1.0
Fat	4.0

You can make these and freeze them, but allow them to cool first. When thawed just heat through, covered with foil, in a warm oven.

Potato Pancakes

Serves 6 (2 pancakes per serving)

Here are some of the different toppings you could try:
- slices of smoked salmon topped with chive soy cream cheese and decorated with whole chives
- warm crispy bacon and sun-dried tomatoes sprinkled on a dollop of chive soy cream cheese
- quick-fried diced smoked salmon, capers and parsley
- for the vegan, try roasting garlic, peppers and eggplant
- mushrooms tossed in garlic, parsley and olive oil.

3 cups	quartered potatoes (weight peeled 10 oz)	280 g
3/4 cup	soy cream	180 ml
2 tbsps	vegan margarine	50 g
3½ tbsps	all-purpose flour	3½ tbsps
4	eggs, beaten	4
	oil for frying	
	salt, pepper and nutmeg	

Steam or boil potatoes until tender but not wet and mushy. Drain well.

In a large bowl, mash the hot potatoes with the soy cream and margarine until smooth.

Beat in the sifted flour and eggs, which should result in a thick pouring consistency. Season well with salt, pepper and nutmeg.

Heat a large lightly oiled non-stick frying pan.

Drop about half a ladle full of the mixture into the frying pan. It should spread slightly; make as many pancakes as you can fit in the pan.

Cook for about 1 minute, turn and heat the other side. They should be golden and spongy to touch when cooked.

Serve warm with different toppings. Makes about 12.

PER SERVING	
Calories	172
% Calories from fat	49
Fat (g)	9.3
Saturated fat (g)	1.8
Cholesterol (mg)	141.7
Sodium (mg)	96
Protein (g)	6.2
Carbohydrate (g)	15.1
Calcium (mg)	27.1

EXCHANGES	
Milk	0.0
Vegetable	0.0
Fruit	0.0
Bread	1.0
Meat	0.0
Fat	2.0

Many of the ingredients may be changed for a different variation. Mushrooms could be used instead of eggplant. Cashew nuts or Brazil nuts could be used instead of the hazelnuts. Yellow split peas could be used instead of the lentils.

Eggplant and Red Lentil Loaf

Serves 4–6

Savory loaves made out of nuts and legumes were one of the first dishes introduced when vegetarianism became popular. They are not really so popular now, as many other more sophisticated vegetarian dishes are the fashion. However, this type of loaf is very nutritious and often very tasty.

This loaf has the interesting addition of spices and eggplant as well as the nuts and legumes. I find the eggplant prevents the loaf from being too dry. Made in advance, it reheats very well, or have it cold the next day with a tomato salad and mixed greens and perhaps some warm brown rice. If serving this loaf hot, try serving it with the Tomato and Pimiento Coulis on page 121 and the Cucumber, Mint and Soy Yogurt Salad on page 134.

²/₃ cup	dried red lentils	150 g
2	medium onions, finely chopped	2
2 tbsps	olive oil	30 ml
1	small eggplant, cut into small cubes	1
2	cloves garlic, crushed	2
1 tbsp	mild curry powder	1 tbsp
1 tsp	cumin powder	1 tsp
1 tsp	turmeric	1 tsp
¹/₂ tsp	cilantro powder	¹/₂ tsp
1 tsp	vegan bouillon powder	1 tsp
¹/₂ cup	breadcrumbs	110 g
2 oz	hazelnuts, finely chopped	56 g
1	egg, beaten	1
2 tbsps	chopped fresh cilantro	2 tbsps
	salt and freshly ground pepper	

Pre-heat the oven to 350F. Grease and line the base of a 1 quart loaf pan.

Rinse the lentils and tip into a small saucepan. Cover with plenty of water, bring to a boil then simmer for 8–10 minutes until tender; drain and leave to dry out.

In a large saucepan, sauté the onion in the olive oil for about 3 minutes.

Add the eggplant and garlic, and continue cooking, stirring well, for about 6 minutes until soft.

VEGETARIAN

PER SERVING

Calories	399
% Calories from fat	40
Fat (g)	18.4
Saturated fat (g)	2.3
Cholesterol (mg)	53.1
Sodium (mg)	389
Protein (g)	16.9
Carbohydrate (g)	45.8
Calcium (mg)	106.6

EXCHANGES

Milk	0.0
Vegetable	0.0
Fruit	0.0
Bread	3.0
Meat	1.0
Fat	3.0

Stir in the curry powder, cumin, turmeric, cilantro and bouillon and sauté for several minutes to cook the spices.

Mix in the lentils, breadcrumbs and hazelnuts, until well blended.

Add the beaten egg and fresh cilantro and season well.

Pour into the prepared loaf pan and smooth down.

Bake for about 40 minutes until the top is crisp and golden and the loaf feels firm to the touch in the center. Insert a toothpick in the center of the loaf, and if it comes out very wet, cook longer.

Allow to cool for a few minutes, then turn out onto a warm plate to serve.

Larger field mushrooms have a more intense flavor than the small cup variety.

Baked Stuffed Mushrooms

Serves 4 (4 mushrooms per serving)

This is one of my favorite vegetarian dishes, especially as it is so incredibly easy to prepare with the mushrooms requiring no pre-cooking. They can be made in advance and cooked when required.

This would also be suitable as part of a buffet lunch or as a starter, using small mushrooms.

Delicious served with the Roasted Tomato Sauce on page 119 and a green salad, or as a hot main meal with the Tomato and Pimiento Coulis on page 121.

16	large brown or white mushrooms	16
1	large onion, finely chopped	1
1 tbsp	olive oil	15 ml
3	cloves garlic, crushed	3
2	ribs celery, finely chopped	2
1/2 cup	breadcrumbs	110 g
1	bunch parsley (the greener, the tastier the stuffing)	1
2	sprigs fresh thyme	2
2 oz	flaked almonds (2 tbsps)	56 g
1/2 cup	soy cheese	110 g
	salt and freshly ground pepper	
	a little extra olive oil to drizzle	

VEGAN

PER SERVING	
Calories	247
% Calories from fat	51
Fat (g)	14.8
Saturated fat (g)	1.6
Cholesterol (mg)	0
Sodium (mg)	242
Protein (g)	11.1
Carbohydrate (g)	20.8
Calcium (mg)	190.1

EXCHANGES	
Milk	0.0
Vegetable	1.0
Fruit	0.0
Bread	1.0
Meat	1.0
Fat	2.0

Pre-heat the oven to 375F. Wipe the mushrooms and remove the stalks; place the mushrooms in a suitable baking dish.

In a large frying pan, sauté the onion in the olive oil over medium heat for about 5 minutes until fairly soft.

Stir in the garlic and celery and sauté gently for a further 4 minutes, stirring regularly.

If making breadcrumbs in a processor, add the herbs while processing the bread. If you already have breadcrumbs, chop the herbs finely and mix them with the breadcrumbs.

Under the broiler, grill the flaked almonds until golden, turning regularly to prevent them from blackening.

In a large bowl, combine the breadcrumbs, onion mixture and almonds. Then crumble or grate in the soy cheese; mix well and season.

If the mixture seems very dry, add an extra tablespoon of olive oil to moisten it (this will hold it together better for stuffing).

Fill the mushrooms, packing the mixture in well, and drizzle with extra olive oil.

Bake in the oven for about 20–25 minutes until the mushrooms are soft and the tops are golden brown. Transfer to warm plates to serve.

Some washed and finely sliced spinach could be stirred into the hot mixture just before serving.

Garam masala is an Indian spice that may be found in ethnic aisles or at Indian grocery stores.

PER SERVING	
Calories	437
% Calories from fat	22
Fat (g)	11.4
Saturated fat (g)	1.2
Cholesterol (mg)	0
Sodium (mg)	634
Protein (g)	15.3
Carbohydrate (g)	73.2
Calcium (mg)	173.2

EXCHANGES	
Milk	0.0
Vegetable	0.0
Fruit	0.0
Bread	0.0
Meat	0.0
Fat	0.0

Chick Peas with Tomatoes and Cilantro

Serves 2–3

This is a nutritious and satisfying dish using chick peas, which have a distinctive nutty flavor and are one of the most versatile beans. I sometimes like to cook them so they are slightly more crunchy than the canned variety, although having a can available in the cupboard is extremely handy. Serve this with brown rice and a crisp salad or as an accompaniment to Indian dishes.

1 tbsp	vegetable oil	15 ml
1	medium onion, finely chopped	1
3	cloves garlic, crushed	3
2	small green chili peppers, de-seeded and finely chopped	2
1/2 tsp	ground paprika	1/2 tsp
1 tsp	ground cumin	1 tsp
1 tsp	ground cilantro	1 tsp
1/2 tsp	garam masala	1/2 tsp
4	large ripe tomatoes, roughly chopped	4
1 tsp	brown sugar	8 g
1	14-oz can of chick peas, drained (about 2 cups cooked from dried)	1
2 tbsps	chopped fresh cilantro	2 tbsps
	salt and pepper	

Heat the oil in a medium saucepan, add the onion and sauté gently for about 4 minutes.

Stir in the garlic, chilies and spices and continue cooking for several minutes.

Next, add the tomatoes and sugar, and simmer gently for about 10 minutes until tomatoes turn to a purée.

Stir in the chick peas and the fresh cilantro and heat for about 3 minutes until chick peas are heated through.

Season well and serve in a warm dish.

Try to use free-range eggs whenever possible.

Curried Spinach and Eggs

Serves 4

This is a very tasty, quick and nutritious supper. Serve hot with either brown rice or hot Indian naan bread.

10 cups	fresh spinach or 10 oz pkg frozen leaf spinach	280 g
1 tbsp	peanut oil	15 ml
1	medium onion, finely chopped	1
2	cloves garlic, crushed	2
1 tsp	black mustard seeds	1 tsp
2 tsps	medium curry powder	2 tsps
1 tsp	turmeric	1 tsp
1/2 tsp	chili powder	1/2 tsp
1 cup	vegetable stock	240 ml
1/2 cup	low-fat coconut milk	120 ml
	salt and freshly ground pepper	
	pinch of nutmeg	
1 tbsp	chopped fresh cilantro	1 tbsp
6	fresh eggs	6

Wash and prepare spinach. Put into a pan without water, cover and cook gently (or you could steam it above some rice). After about 5 minutes the spinach will have reduced by two-thirds (it should be just under-cooked).

Drain, rinse with cold water to retain color, squeeze all water out and roughly chop.

In a large frying pan, heat the oil and sauté onion and garlic for about 5 minutes until soft. Add the mustard seeds and powdered spices and cook, stirring well, for a further 5 minutes.

Next, mix in the stock and coconut milk and bring to a boil. Stir in the spinach, season, heat through and keep warm.

Put the eggs in a small saucepan of cold water, bring up to a boil, then gently simmer for 6–7 minutes until just hard boiled. Remove shells, and cut in half while still hot.

Serve spinach in a large warm dish and place the halved eggs on top. Sprinkle with cilantro to serve.

VEGETARIAN

PER SERVING

Calories	203
% Calories from fat	59
Fat (g)	13.4
Saturated fat (g)	4
Cholesterol (mg)	318.7
Sodium (mg)	334
Protein (g)	13
Carbohydrate (g)	8.2
Calcium (mg)	123.4

EXCHANGES

Milk	0.0
Vegetable	2.0
Fruit	0.0
Bread	0.0
Meat	1.0
Fat	2.0

I often cook this with any combination of fillings, such as peppers, mushrooms, ham, bacon, broccoli, asparagus, etc.

Potato, Bean and Corn Frittata

Serves 4

A frittata is an open Italian omelette. Unlike many omelettes, which may be creamy or runny, a frittata is set firm but not stiff and dry. It is not folded as is a conventional omelette, but consists of a single thin layer at the bottom of the pan in which it is made. Also, the filling ingredients are added to the eggs while they are uncooked, and the frittata is then cooked slowly over a low heat.

1 tbsp	olive oil	15 ml
4	green onions, washed and sliced	4
1	clove garlic, crushed	1
2 cups	cooked, diced new potatoes (1/2 lb)	225 g
3/4 cup	cooked fresh sweetcorn (scraped off the cob)	165 g
1/2 cup	stringbeans, blanched and refreshed, cut into 1/2-inch lengths (about 4 oz)	112 g
6	eggs, beaten and seasoned with salt and pepper	6
1 tbsp	chopped fresh parsley	1 tbsp
1 tbsp	vegan margarine	25 g

Using a large, heavy-based omelette pan, heat the oil and gently sauté the green onions, garlic and new potatoes for about 8 minutes until the potatoes begin to turn golden. Then add in the sweetcorn and the beans and mix well.

Break the eggs into a large bowl and whisk until well blended; stir in the parsley.

Tip the vegetables from the pan into the eggs, and mix thoroughly until all the ingredients are well combined. Pre-heat the broiler.

Wipe out the omelette pan, then gently heat the margarine until it is beginning to foam but not burning.

Tip in the egg and vegetable mixture and smooth down. Cook over low to medium heat for about 8 minutes until the eggs have set and only the surface is runny.

Place the pan under the hot broiler and cook the top for about 3 minutes until golden and slightly risen.

Cut into 4 large wedges, and slide each onto a serving dish to serve.

VEGETARIAN

PER SERVING

Calories	270
% Calories from fat	45
Fat (g)	14
Saturated fat (g)	3.4
Cholesterol (mg)	318.7
Sodium (mg)	137
Protein (g)	12.2
Carbohydrate (g)	25.1
Calcium (mg)	65.9

EXCHANGES

Milk	0.0
Vegetable	0.0
Fruit	0.0
Bread	2.0
Meat	1.0
Fat	2.0

There are two readily available varieties of sweet potato, one being bright orange inside when cooked, the other yellow with a chestnut flavor. Either sort would be suitable.

Sweet Potato and Chick Pea Cakes

Serves 4 (2 cakes per serving)

These crispy cakes are packed with flavor and goodness. They are ideal as a meal on their own or as a side dish. Serve hot with Tomato and Sweet Chili Relish (see page 122) and perhaps the Cucumber, Mint and Soy Yogurt Salad (see page 134).

1	large or 2 smaller sweet potatoes (about 1 lb)	1
1	medium onion, finely chopped	1
1	small leek, washed, finely chopped	1
3	cloves garlic, crushed	3
3 tbsps	vegetable oil	45 ml
1 tsp	vegan bouillon powder	1 tsp
1	green chili pepper, chopped finely, seeds discarded (optional)	1
1 1/2 tsps	ground cumin	1 1/2 tsps
1/2 tsp	ground cilantro	1/2 tsp
1/2 tsp	ground turmeric	1/2 tsp
1	14-oz can chick peas, drained (about 2 cups cooked from dried)	1
	salt and freshly ground pepper	
1 tbsp	all-purpose flour	1 tbsp
1 tbsp	sesame seeds	1 tbsp

Pre-heat the oven to 350F. Peel, cube and steam or boil sweet potato for 10–15 minutes until soft.

Drain well and, using a potato masher, mash until smooth.

Sauté the onion, leek and garlic in a frying pan in 1 table-spoon oil for about 15 minutes over medium heat, until soft.

Add the bouillon powder, chili and spices into the pan, stir well and continue cooking for 2 minutes.

In a large bowl, mash the chick peas, leaving them slightly chunky.

Add the onion mixture and sweet potatoes to the chick peas, combining well.

Season with salt and pepper, and leave to cool slightly.

On a large plate, mix the flour with the sesame seeds.

VEGAN

PER SERVING	
Calories	386
% Calories from fat	30
Fat (g)	13.1
Saturated fat (g)	1.7
Cholesterol (mg)	0
Sodium (mg)	566
Protein (g)	8.6
Carbohydrate (g)	60
Calcium (mg)	112.8

EXCHANGES	
Milk	0.0
Vegetable	0.0
Fruit	0.0
Bread	4.0
Meat	0.0
Fat	2.0

Divide the potato mixture into 8 and shape into round cakes about 1 inch thick. Roll each cake in the flour and sesame seeds.

In a large, clean frying pan, heat the remaining oil and fry the cakes for 4 minutes on each side over medium heat until golden.

Place on a baking sheet and finish off in the oven for 10 minutes until heated through.

Main Dishes—Fish, Meat and Vegetarian

Spicy Fillet of Beef Stroganoff

Rich Braised Beef

Seared Calves' Liver with Bacon and Wine Sauce

Chili Chicken with Basil and Coconut

Creole Chicken

Chicken Casseroled in Cider with Mushrooms and Mustard

Chicken and Mushroom Pie

Chicken Breasts with Mushroom, Bacon and Tarragon Sauce

Duck Breast with Orange and Red Wine Sauce

Roasted Leg of Duck with Ginger and Honey

Lamb Hot Pot with Pearl Barley

Marinated Lamb Kebabs

Lamb Tagine

Pork Steak with Hazelnut and Sage Crust

Fillet of Trout, East Indian Style

Grilled Fillet of Trout with Watercress Sauce

Fish, Shrimp and Leek Pie

Cajun Blackened Fish

Pan-Fried Tuna Steaks with Salsa Verde

Broiled Catfish with Soy, Honey and Horseradish Dressing

Crusted Fillet of Cod

Monkfish and Shrimp Brochettes

Crunchy Oat-Coated Mahi-Mahi Fillets

Potato-Crusted Haddock and Curried Tomato Bake

Smoked Fish Cakes

Smoked Trout Rarebit

Split Pea and Vegetable Pot Pie

Individual Mushroom and Walnut Strudels

This dish is also delicious made with pork fillet and more economical. If using pork fillet, cut in strips. They will need to be cooked slightly longer to ensure the pork is thoroughly cooked through, whereas beef fillet can be served slightly pink.

Spicy Fillet of Beef Stroganoff

Serves 4

This classic stroganoff is made with thin strips of beef fillet, which are cooked very quickly. I added cayenne to give it a bit of a kick! Serve this stroganoff with rice and some green vegetables.

1 lb	beef fillet mignon or tenderloin	450 g
½ lb	small button mushrooms, wiped	225 g
1½ tbsp	vegan margarine	37 g
1	medium onion, halved and thinly sliced	1
1¼ tsp	cayenne pepper	1¼ tsp
1 cup	(scant) dry white wine or dry cider	240 ml
1 cup	(scant) good beef stock (chicken stock will also do)	240 ml
½ tbsp	vegetable oil	8 ml
3 tbsps	brandy	45 ml
3 tbsps	soy cream	45 ml
	salt and freshly ground black pepper	
	freshly ground nutmeg	
1 tbsp	chopped parsley	1 tbsp

Cut the beef fillet into thin strips ¼ inch wide, ¼ inch thick and 2½ inches long. Trim the stalks and slice the mushrooms. Melt the margarine in a frying pan over medium heat, and cook the onion for about 5 minutes until soft.

Stir in the mushrooms and 1 teaspoon cayenne, increase the heat and cook for about 2 minutes.

Pour the wine over the mushrooms and allow to boil for a few seconds, then add the stock. Continue simmering until the liquid is about half the initial amount. Pour out into a bowl.

Heat the oil in a large, clean, heavy frying pan as hot as possible without burning. Drop in the beef strips.

Shake and toss over a fast heat to brown and seal the edges without overcooking in the middle. Take pan off the heat. Remove beef strips from pan.

Pour the brandy into the fairly hot pan. Set light to the brandy and when flames die down, pour in mushroom and stock mixture. Return the meat and allow to heat through for several minutes. Gently stir in 2 tablespoons of the soy cream, add salt and pepper and a good grating of fresh nutmeg. Serve in a warm serving dish.

Drizzle top with remaining soy cream and sprinkle the remaining ¼ teaspoon of cayenne over the soy cream. Finely sprinkle the chopped parsley over the beef.

PER SERVING	
Calories	459
% Calories from fat	64
Fat (g)	30.1
Saturated fat (g)	10.4
Cholesterol (mg)	77.5
Sodium (mg)	608
Protein (g)	23.2
Carbohydrate (g)	6.8
Calcium (mg)	25.3

EXCHANGES	
Milk	0.0
Vegetable	1.0
Fruit	0.0
Bread	0.0
Meat	3.0
Fat	6.0

Rich Braised Beef

Serves 6

This is a wonderful way of cooking tougher cuts of meat and fairly easy to make. I quite often cook this for friends coming to supper, as it can be prepared well in advance and improves after a day or two. I have used round of beef, which is easy to prepare and has little wastage. Simply slice across in steak-like pieces, which looks much nicer than a casserole with small cubes of meat. Serve with baked or new potatoes, and the sauce from the pan will be enough to make them delicious without the need to add a butter substitute. This dish may be served with rice or potatoes and vegetables.

1½ lb	round of beef	675 g
8 oz	piece of lightly smoked bacon (buy whole from butcher)	225 g
1 tbsp	oil	15 ml
2	medium onions, sliced	2
3	cloves garlic, crushed	3
2	ribs celery, chopped	2
	seasoned flour (all-purpose flour with salt and pepper)	
1	bottle of red wine	750 ml
2 cups	good beef stock	480 ml
	a few sprigs of fresh thyme, stalks removed	
2	bay leaves	2
	salt and pepper	

Pre-heat the oven to 300F. Trim the meat and cut it into steak-like pieces (or ask butcher to do so) about 1 inch thick.

Next trim off the rind and excess fat from the bacon, and cut it into ¼-inch chunks.

Heat 1 teaspoon oil in a large frying pan. Fry the onions, garlic and celery for a few minutes, then tip them into a large, deep casserole dish.

Stir the bacon into the hot pan and fry for 1 minute; tip into the casserole dish with the onions.

Toss the meat in the seasoned flour. Heat remaining oil in the pan and brown the beef pieces very well, a few at a time. Place into the casserole dish when browned.

If the bottom of the pan becomes dark or too dry, remove the beef and pour in a little wine; scrape any sediment stuck on the

PER SERVING	
Calories	543
% Calories from fat	49
Fat (g)	25.4
Saturated fat (g)	8.2
Cholesterol (mg)	96.6
Sodium (mg)	1360
Protein (g)	38.9
Carbohydrate (g)	14.3
Calcium (mg)	37.2
EXCHANGES	
Milk	0.0
Vegetable	0.0
Fruit	0.0
Bread	1.0
Meat	6.0
Fat	3.0

bottom of the pan (this is called deglazing). Pour the pan liquid into the casserole dish. When all the meat is browned, deglaze the pan once more. Pour any remaining wine over the beef in the casserole dish, followed by the stock, thyme and bay leaves.

Cover the casserole dish with aluminum foil. Bake slowly for 3 hours or until meat is tender.

After this time, adjust the sauce by pouring all the liquid into a saucepan, leaving the meat in the casserole dish. Bring the liquid to a boil, and simmer until it has reduced by half and becomes slightly thicker and stronger tasting; season well with salt and pepper. (I sometimes add a dash of dark soy sauce instead of salt, which gives a good dark color to the sauce.) Pour sauce over the meat.

Return to the oven, uncovered, for about 10 minutes. Serve hot from the oven.

When buying calves' liver, it should be milky brown in color with a fine even texture.

Avoid pork liver, except for making pâtés and terrines.

Seared Calves' Liver with Bacon and Wine Sauce

Serves 4

The liver is best served slightly pink in the middle; if overcooked it becomes tougher and darker. Serve with potatoes and green vegetables.

1 tbsp	sunflower oil	15 ml
4	shallots, peeled and finely chopped	4
6	slices smoked back bacon, finely chopped	6
2 tsps	all-purpose flour	2 tsps
1½ tbsps	sherry vinegar	23 ml
½ cup	red wine	120 ml
1 cup	good beef stock	240 ml
1 tsp	chopped fresh sage	1 tsp
1 tsp	sugar	16 g
	salt and freshly ground pepper	
1 lb	calves' liver, ask butcher to slice into 4 slices each about ½ inch thick	450 g

PER SERVING	
Calories	294
% Calories from fat	47
Fat (g)	14.3
Saturated fat (g)	4.3
Cholesterol (mg)	360.6
Sodium (mg)	767
Protein (g)	24.9
Carbohydrate (g)	9.7
Calcium (mg)	27.3
EXCHANGES	
Milk	0.0
Vegetable	0.0
Fruit	0.0
Bread	0.5
Meat	3.0
Fat	2.0

	all-purpose flour for dusting	
	dash of oil for frying	
8	extra sage leaves for garnishing	8

Heat the oil in a small saucepan, and add the shallots and bacon. Cook slowly for 10 to 15 minutes until the shallots are soft and beginning to caramelize.

Sprinkle the flour over the shallots and stir well over medium heat for about half a minute; remove pan from the heat.

Pour in the vinegar and red wine and, stirring well, return to the heat.

Add the stock, sage and sugar and bring to a boil, then simmer for 5 minutes until the sauce thickens slightly. Season well.

To cook the calves' liver, heat a large, heavy frying pan, brushed with oil, to a high temperature.

Lightly dust the liver with some extra flour, and season with pepper.

Place the liver on the hot pan for about 2 minutes until the heat has cooked the liver through almost to the top.

Quickly flip over the liver, and cook briefly on the other side before serving browned underside up on warmed plates.

Reheat the sauce and carefully pour over the liver.

Garnish each portion with 2 fresh sage leaves and serve immediately.

An alternative to Chinese 5 spice powder is Thai 7 spice seasoning. It contains chili powder, garlic, cilantro powder, ground lemon peel, cinnamon, cumin, star anise, onion powder, jalapeño powder and cloves. If you cannot find it, use a combination of these spices from your cupboard.

For a vegan dish, omit the chicken and try using sautéed mushrooms, eggplant and chick peas. Be sure to use soy sauce and not fish sauce.

Chili Chicken with Basil and Coconut

Serves 4

This Thai-style chicken stir-fry is very quick and easy to prepare and makes a delicious meal served with Thai fragrant rice and salad.

Coconut milk, although fairly sweet, is a great addition to the lactose-free diet, as it not only contains some calcium but also gives dishes a lovely creamy taste. It is particularly good in Thai-style dishes, which have a hot and sweet taste.

4	chicken breast fillets (about 4 oz each)	4
2 tbsps	peanut oil	30 ml
1	onion, finely chopped	1
1	red chili pepper, de-seeded and finely sliced	1
1	red bell pepper, de-seeded and finely diced	1
2 tsps	Chinese 5 spice powder	2 tsps
2 tsps	chili sauce	2 tsps
2 tbsps	fish sauce or soy sauce	30 ml
1	large bunch fresh basil, shredded (save a few leaves for garnishing)	1
1	14-oz can coconut milk	1

Skin the chicken breasts and cut into $1/2$-inch strips.

Heat a wok with the oil and quickly stir-fry the onion, chili and bell peppers for about 2 minutes, stirring constantly.

Stir in the chicken strips and 5 spice seasoning and sauté for about 3 minutes until chicken is tender.

Pour the chili sauce and fish sauce over the chicken and cook for a further minute.

Stir in the shredded basil leaves and the coconut milk, and simmer gently until well heated through.

Serve in a warmed dish.

PER SERVING	
Calories	462
% Calories from fat	64
Fat (g)	33.7
Saturated fat (g)	23.8
Cholesterol (mg)	65.7
Sodium (mg)	813
Protein (g)	30.2
Carbohydrate (g)	12.7
Calcium (mg)	60.6

EXCHANGES	
Milk	1.0
Vegetable	0.0
Fruit	0.0
Bread	0.0
Meat	3.0
Fat	5.0

Also delicious made with fillet of fish, shrimp or fillet of pork.

Creole Chicken

Serves 4

This Cajun-style dish has a rich and spicy flavor. The fiery heat of the dish is mellowed down by the addition of soy cream. Serve with the Spicy Potato Wedges on page 105 or with plain rice.

2 tbsps	all-purpose flour	2 tbsps
2 tbsps	sweet paprika	2 tbsps
2 tbsps	Cajun spice	2 tbsps
4	chicken breasts (about 4 oz each)	4
2 tbsps	olive oil	30 ml
1	large onion, chopped	1
2	cloves garlic, crushed	2
1	large red bell pepper (or 2 small), de-seeded, halved and sliced	1
1³/₄ cups	vegetable or chicken stock	420 ml
1 cup	(scant) soy cream	240 ml
¹/₂ tsp	dried basil	¹/₂ tsp

Mix the flour, paprika and Cajun spice on a large plate. Skin the chicken breasts and cut them into large chunks; roll them in the spiced flour mixture.

Heat a medium saucepan with 1 tablespoon oil. Sauté the onion, garlic and bell peppers for about 5 minutes over medium heat.

As soon as the onions are beginning to soften, tip the remaining spiced flour mixture into the pan. Cook gently for about a minute, stirring well.

Remove the pan from the heat and gradually add the stock. Return the sauce to the heat, bring to a boil, stirring constantly, and cook for about 1 minute until the sauce thickens.

Heat a large frying pan with the remaining oil. Sear the chicken pieces for several minutes on either side until golden.

Pour the sauce over the chicken and simmer for about 4 minutes.

Stir in the soy cream and basil and gently heat through. Serve the chicken on warm plates. Serve immediately.

PER SERVING	
Calories	297
% Calories from fat	40
Fat (g)	13.1
Saturated fat (g)	1.4
Cholesterol (mg)	65.7
Sodium (mg)	519
Protein (g)	28.6
Carbohydrate (g)	14.9
Calcium (mg)	32.6

EXCHANGES	
Milk	0.0
Vegetable	0.0
Fruit	0.0
Bread	1.0
Meat	3.0
Fat	1.0

Rather than cutting up a whole chicken, you may find it easier to use pre-cut chicken thighs and drumsticks. This also allows you to choose better quality chicken—the thighs and legs of organic or free-range chicken are often much cheaper than the breast. Allow for one whole thigh per person.

Chicken Casseroled in Cider with Mushrooms and Mustard

Serves 4–5

This delicious rich casserole could be served with a crisp jacket potato, steamed potatoes or brown rice. The addition of a mild variety of mustard blends with the stock and cider to give a rich, creamy sauce without the addition of a cream substitute. This casserole may be prepared a day or two in advance. It is also suitable for freezing so long as the chicken has not been previously frozen.

4 lb	roasting chicken, skin removed	1.8 kg
1 tbsp	all-purpose flour seasoned with salt and pepper	1 tbsp
2 tbsps	vegetable oil	30 ml
1	onion, finely chopped	1
1¼ cups	button mushrooms, halved (7 oz)	196 g
1¼ cups	dry cider (white wine could also be used)	300 ml
3 tbsps	Dijon mustard (mild variety)	3 tbsps
1¼ cups	chicken stock (preferably made earlier using chicken carcass)	300 ml
2	sprigs fresh thyme	2
1 tbsp	chopped parsley	1 tbsp

Pre-heat the oven to 375F. Cut-up the chicken into 8 pieces, and roll the pieces in the seasoned flour.

Heat a large frying pan with 1 tablespoon oil, and brown the pieces for approximately 4 minutes on either side. Remove the chicken pieces from the pan, and place in suitable oven casserole dish.

Heat the remaining oil and sauté the onion and mushrooms for about 4 minutes. Sprinkle over the remaining plain flour and stir well. Gradually pour in the cider and mustard, stirring well, and bring to a boil. Stir in the stock, mixing well, bring to a boil and allow to simmer for several minutes. Season with extra salt and freshly ground pepper if necessary, and add the thyme leaves pulled off their stalks. Pour this sauce over the browned chicken pieces.

Cover with foil and bake in the oven for about 1 hour until tender. Remove from the oven; the sauce should be the consistency of single cream. Garnish with chopped parsley before serving.

PER SERVING	
Calories	474
% Calories from fat	34
Fat (g)	16.8
Saturated fat (g)	3.4
Cholesterol (mg)	211
Sodium (mg)	588
Protein (g)	61.2
Carbohydrate (g)	7.7
Calcium (mg)	58.5

EXCHANGES	
Milk	0.0
Vegetable	0.0
Fruit	0.5
Bread	0.0
Meat	8.0
Fat	0.0

This same dish can be done with rabbit or pheasant instead of chicken.

Also you could just roast legs and thighs for this dish and save the breast, which would make it more economical.

Wait until the filling is cold before topping with pastry.

Chicken and Mushroom Pie

Serves 4

This traditional pie is perfect for a cold winter's day. It can be prepared in advance and kept chilled with the uncooked pastry top. Serve with some steamed Brussell's sprouts or spring greens.

2 tbsps	sunflower oil	30 ml
1	onion, finely chopped	1
2 tbsps	all-purpose flour	2 tbsps
1¼ cups	good strong chicken stock	300 ml
½ cup	soy milk	120 ml
1 tsp	chopped fresh tarragon or ½ teaspoon dried tarragon	1 tsp
1 tsp	Dijon mustard	1 tsp
	salt and freshly ground pepper	
¼ cup	soy cream	60 ml
3 lb	whole chicken, poached, skinned, boned and cut into large chunks	1.35 kg
1½ cups	button mushrooms, wiped and sliced (8 oz)	225 g
1 recipe	Shortcrust Pastry (see page 187)	1 recipe
	1 beaten egg mixed with pinch of salt and 1 teaspoon water (egg wash)	

Pre-heat the oven to 375F. Heat 1 tablespoon of oil in a large saucepan and sauté the onion for about 8 minutes until soft but not brown.

Remove the pan from heat, and stir in the flour. Return to a low heat and cook for 2 minutes until the flour is a pale golden brown.

Remove the pan from the heat, and gradually blend in the chicken stock.

Return once more to medium heat, and stir until you have a thick, shiny sauce.

Pour in the soy milk, stirring well, and gently bring the sauce to a boil.

Stir in the tarragon, mustard, seasoning and soy cream, and simmer for 2 minutes. Taste and add more seasoning if necessary. Allow to cool.

In a clean frying pan, heat up the remaining oil. When hot, quickly sauté the mushrooms for about 4 minutes until just cooked. Allow to cool slightly.

PER SERVING	
Calories	771
% Calories from fat	46
Fat (g)	38.1
Saturated fat (g)	9.2
Cholesterol (mg)	249.7
Sodium (mg)	450
Protein (g)	69.5
Carbohydrate (g)	33.3
Calcium (mg)	60.5
EXCHANGES	
Milk	0.0
Vegetable	0.0
Fruit	0.0
Bread	2.0
Meat	9.0
Fat	3.0

Roll the pastry on a floured board into a large ¼-inch-thick oval. Using an upturned oval pie dish, in which you will be baking the pie, cut around the pastry rim, making a lid for the pie.

Tip the mushrooms and the chicken into the sauce, mix well and then pour into the pie dish.

Wet the edge of the pastry and lift it, wet side down, onto the pie.

Use any leftover pastry to decorate the top of the pie if you wish.

Prick the top with a fork several times. Brush with beaten egg.

Bake for about 30 minutes, until the pastry top is golden and risen and the pie is well heated through.

This dish could be made with pheasant or guinea fowl breast.

Chicken Breasts with Mushroom, Bacon and Tarragon Sauce

Serves 4

This sauce makes a plain chicken breast into something rich and exotic. The peppercorns give an interesting spicy addition. Ideal served with rice or potatoes.

2 tbsps	olive oil	30 ml
4	chicken breasts, excess fat and skin removed	4
1	large onion, peeled, halved and sliced	1
2–3 slices	unsmoked bacon, finely chopped	2–3 slices
1½ cups	mushrooms, thinly sliced (8 oz)	225 g
½ cup	dry white wine	120 ml
2 tsps	chopped fresh tarragon	2 tsps
1 cup	(scant) vegetable or chicken stock	220 ml
1 cup	(scant) soy cream	220 ml
	salt and freshly ground pepper	

PER SERVING	
Calories	315
% Calories from fat	43
Fat (g)	14.4
Saturated fat (g)	2
Cholesterol (mg)	69.1
Sodium (mg)	271
Protein (g)	29
Carbohydrate (g)	9.5
Calcium (mg)	28.2
EXCHANGES	
Milk	0.0
Vegetable	1.0
Fruit	0.0
Bread	0.0
Meat	4.0
Fat	2.0

Pre-heat the oven to 350F. Heat a large non-stick frying pan with 1 tablespoon of the olive oil. When hot, add chicken breasts and sear for about 1 minute on each side until golden brown.

Place in an oven dish and bake for 15–20 minutes. Meanwhile, add the remaining olive oil to the frying pan and sauté the onion for about 5 minutes until just soft.

Add the bacon and mushrooms and, stirring well, continue cooking for a further 5 minutes.

Pour in the wine, tarragon and stock and bring to a boil; cook for about 4 minutes.

Lastly, add the soy cream, stir well and season, then warm over low heat.

Remove chicken from the oven and slice each breast in half on a diagonal. The meat should be white throughout; if any pinkness remains, cook the chicken longer.

When the chicken is done, arrange it on warm plates and spoon over the sauce.

Slashing the duck breast helps to cook it evenly and also releases more of the fat. Leaving the duck breast to rest for 5 minutes before carving will make the meat more tender.

Duck Breast with Orange and Red Wine Sauce

Serves 6

Duck breasts are increasingly easy to find nowadays and extremely popular with most people. They are best cooked at a higher temperature for a short time and served slightly pink in the middle.

This is a great dish when you want to serve something special. Make the sauce in advance and reheat to serve. Delicious served with the Potato and Celeriac Boulangère (see page 102), or try with the Stir-Fried Cabbage and Carrots with Caraway (see page 98).

1 tbsp	vegetable oil	15 ml
1	large onion, sliced	1
3	ribs of celery, chopped	3
2/3 cup	chopped mushroom stalks (4 oz)	112 g
1	carrot, sliced	1
1 1/4 cups	red wine	300 ml
2 1/2 cups	chicken stock	600 ml
	sprig of thyme	
2	bay leaves	2
1/2 cup	orange juice	120 ml
	zest of one orange	
4	duck breasts, trim excess fat (6 oz each)	4
	salt and freshly ground pepper	

Pre-heat the oven to 425F. In a large saucepan, heat the oil and cook the onion, celery, mushroom stalks and carrot for about 10 minutes until they begin to brown but not burn.

Pour in the red wine to deglaze the pan, and allow to boil for a few seconds.

Next, add the stock and herbs and simmer uncovered for about 30 minutes, until it has reduced by about two-thirds.

Pass everything through a fine sieve, and put back the gravy along with the orange juice and zest. Set aside until you begin to cook the duck.

PER SERVING	
Calories	563
% Calories from fat	41
Fat (g)	25.1
Saturated fat (g)	6.5
Cholesterol (mg)	313.1
Sodium (mg)	326
Protein (g)	65.1
Carbohydrate (g)	7.8
Calcium (mg)	45.2

EXCHANGES	
Milk	0.0
Vegetable	1.0
Fruit	0.0
Bread	0.0
Meat	9.0
Fat	1.0

Slash the skin of the duck diagonally about 4 times on each breast, and season with salt and pepper.

Heat a large pan (preferably one with oven-proof handles) until hot, and add duck breasts skin side up.

Cook for 2 minutes, then turn skin side down and cook for a further 2 minutes.

Pour off excess duck fat, and put duck breasts in the oven for a further 10 minutes. Remove from oven and allow to rest for 5 minutes.

Meanwhile, return the sauce to the stove, bring to a boil and simmer for about 5 minutes until it begins to thicken slightly.

Pour any excess juices (not the fat) from the duck breasts into the sauce.

Slice each duck breast into about 4 diagonal slices, and place slices on a warm plate. Pour over the hot sauce before serving.

Chicken legs could be used instead of duck.

Roasted Leg of Duck with Ginger and Honey

Serves 4

Duck legs are often the most affordable way of buying duck. As with chicken legs, duck legs benefit from a longer, slower roasting time, and as a result, they will be tender and well cooked. For this recipe I have slashed the duck legs prior to marinating, which allows the spices to infuse into the duck, and this, along with the ginger and honey, gives the duck a delicious oriental taste. The longer you can marinate the duck legs, the more the flavor will develop. Serve with Sesame Noodles on page 107 and some stir-fry vegetables.

4	duck legs, about 2½ oz each, skin removed	4
4 tsps	Chinese 5 spice powder	4 tsps
1 inch	fresh gingerroot, peeled and very finely chopped	2.5 cm
¼ cup	honey	¼ cup
4 tsps	dark soy sauce	20 ml
4 tsps	light soy sauce	20 ml

Slash the duck legs with a sharp knife and rub them over with the Chinese 5 spice.

Lay the duck legs in an oven-proof dish and allow to marinate in the fridge for 3 hours or overnight.

Pre-heat the oven to 350F. Place the duck legs in the oven for 40 minutes until well cooked through. Remove from the oven, and drain off any surrounding fat.

In a small bowl, mix together the ginger, honey and the light and dark soy sauces. Drizzle over duck legs and serve.

PER SERVING	
Calories	213
% Calories from fat	20
Fat (g)	4.6
Saturated fat (g)	1
Cholesterol (mg)	78.7
Sodium (mg)	619
Protein (g)	22.7
Carbohydrate (g)	19.7
Calcium (mg)	31.1
EXCHANGES	
Milk	0.0
Vegetable	0.0
Fruit	1.0
Bread	0.0
Meat	3.0
Fat	0.0

For variety, place a layer of thinly sliced peeled potato on the top 40 minutes before the end of the cooking time.

Lamb Hot Pot with Pearl Barley

Serves 8

This rustic dish contains almost all the ingredients for a complete meal, although perhaps a baked potato served alongside to mop up all the juice would make it more complete! I have used pearl barley, which provides a good source of calcium as well as an interesting nutty flavor to the dish. By cooking the meat on the bone, it remains more succulent and tender.

2½ lb	lean shoulder cut of lamb	1.125 kg
3½ cups	good stock (beef, lamb or chicken)	840 ml
1	large onion, sliced	1
3	ribs celery, cut into ½-inch chunks	3
5	carrots, cut into 1-inch chunks	5
3	bay leaves	3
1	sprig of fresh rosemary	1
3 tbsps	pearl barley	75 g
	salt and freshly ground pepper	

Pre-heat the oven to 350F. Cut the meat into chops, trimming away excess fat.

Heat a heavy pan without oil (as the lamb is naturally quite fatty), and sauté the lamb to brown all sides of it.

Place the browned lamb chops into a large casserole dish.

Deglaze the pan with a splash of the stock, scraping the bottom of the pan to remove all the sediment.

Place the onion, celery, carrot and herbs in the casserole dish with the lamb.

Pour over the stock and pearl barley. Season and cover with aluminum foil.

Place in oven and cook for 2 hours (remove foil after 1 hour, and continue cooking uncovered). The lamb should be tender and beginning to fall away from the bone. Check the sauce for seasoning.

Serve hot from the casserole dish.

PER SERVING	
Calories	379
% Calories from fat	61
Fat (g)	25.2
Saturated fat (g)	10.6
Cholesterol (mg)	98.7
Sodium (mg)	969
Protein (g)	26.2
Carbohydrate (g)	10.3
Calcium (mg)	45.8

EXCHANGES	
Milk	0.0
Vegetable	0.0
Fruit	0.0
Bread	1.0
Meat	3.0
Fat	3.0

Made into smaller kebabs, it could also be a little starter served with Tomato and Sweet Chili Relish (see page 122).

Don't forget to soak the wooden skewers before threading on the meat to prevent charring.

Marinated Lamb Kebabs

Serves 6

These Middle Eastern-style kebabs remind me of summer barbecues. It is one of my husband's favorite dishes, which I often cook served with Spiced Rice, see page 109, a Tomato and Mint Salsa, see page 120, and a Cucumber, Mint and Soy Yogurt Salad, see page 134, for a perfect combination. In this recipe I have broiled the kebabs; however, they are also perfect for barbecuing.

1½ lb	cubed lean leg of lamb	675 g
3 tbsps	olive oil	45 ml
2 tbsps	soy sauce	30 ml
1	large sprig of rosemary, leaves pulled off the stalk	1
4	cloves garlic, crushed	4
2	red or green bell peppers	2
2	onions	2
12	bay leaves	12
6	wooden or metal skewers	6
1	lemon to garnish	1

In a large bowl, mix the lamb pieces with the olive oil, soy sauce, rosemary and garlic.

Put in the fridge to marinate for 4 hours or more.

Cut peppers and onions into ³/₄-inch squares.

Thread the lamb pieces onto the skewers, alternating each piece of lamb with a square of onion, then pepper; thread 2 bay leaves on each skewer.

Place on high shelf under hot broiler for 4–6 minutes each side, until the outside is well browned and the inside is still slightly pink and juicy.

Serve with wedges of lemon.

PER SERVING	
Calories	315
% Calories from fat	62
Fat (g)	21.6
Saturated fat (g)	7.2
Cholesterol (mg)	75.3
Sodium (mg)	394
Protein (g)	22.3
Carbohydrate (g)	7.9
Calcium (mg)	35.7
EXCHANGES	
Milk	0.0
Vegetable	1.0
Fruit	0.0
Bread	0.0
Meat	3.0
Fat	3.0

Follow the recipe using chicken legs and thighs to make Chicken Tagine.

This dish is equally delicious made with dried apricots.

Lamb Tagine

Serves 8

This Moroccan meat stew derives its name from its traditional round dish with a conical lid resembling a pointed hat. The pieces of meat are slow cooked with spices and either prunes or apricots. The generous quantities of black pepper and spices provide a delicate balance with the sweetness of the fruit. I have used boned shoulder of lamb, although leg of lamb would be equally good. You could serve this dish with the traditional accompaniment of couscous and a crisp salad.

1 cup	pitted dried prunes (8 oz)	225 g
2 lb	boned shoulder of lamb	900 g
1 tbsp	all-purpose flour	1 tbsp
2 tsps	ground cumin	2 tsps
1 tsp	ground cinnamon	1 tsp
2 tsps	ground cilantro	2 tsps
1 tsp	ground black pepper	1 tsp
2 tbsps	vegetable oil	30 ml
1	large onion, finely chopped	1
2	cloves garlic, crushed	2
3 cups	good stock (beef, lamb or chicken)	720 ml
	salt	
1 tbsp	chopped fresh cilantro	1 tbsp

Put the prunes in a small bowl and pour over enough water to cover completely. Leave to soak overnight.

Pre-heat the oven to 325F.

Cut the lamb into large chunks about 2 x 2 inches and remove excess fat, skin and gristle.

On a large plate, mix the flour, cumin, cinnamon, cilantro and pepper. Roll the lamb pieces in the flour mixture, coating well.

Heat a large frying pan with half a tablespoon of oil, and brown half of the lamb pieces. Place lamb pieces in a large casserole dish or a tagine. Brown the rest of the lamb in another half a tablespoon of oil, and place in the dish.

Add remaining 1 tablespoon of oil to the pan with the onion and garlic, cook for about 2 minutes then tip in the remaining flour and spice mixture.

Stir for 1 minute, then gradually pour in half of the stock and mix well.

PER SERVING	
Calories	249
% Calories from fat	33
Fat (g)	9
Saturated fat (g)	2.3
Cholesterol (mg)	73
Sodium (mg)	809
Protein (g)	24.8
Carbohydrate (g)	17
Calcium (mg)	36.7
EXCHANGES	
Milk	0.0
Vegetable	0.0
Fruit	1.0
Bread	0.0
Meat	3.0
Fat	0.0

Pour this sauce and the remaining stock over the lamb, cover with foil and bake for 1½ hours until the meat is tender and beginning to fall apart.

Remove from oven and pour off the liquid into a medium saucepan. Stir the prunes and their soaking liquid into the saucepan. Bring to a boil over medium heat, and reduce until slightly thick; you should have about ¾ pint of liquid.

Season well with salt. Pour over the lamb and either leave to cool until required or reheat in the oven until piping hot, approximately 20 minutes. Sprinkle with fresh cilantro to serve.

Pork Steak with Hazelnut and Sage Crust

Serves 4

In this recipe a simple pork steak is coated in a crisp hazelnut and sage crust, transforming it into something far more exotic. I recommend you make the Cider and Wholegrain Mustard Sauce (see page 115) to complement the pork steak perfectly.

2⅓ cups	hazelnuts (5 oz)	140 g
10	fresh sage leaves	10
4	lean leg of pork steaks, off the bone (4 oz each)	450 g
1 tbsp	all-purpose flour, seasoned with salt and pepper	1 tbsp
1	large egg, beaten	1
1 tbsp	soy milk	15 ml
1 tsp	vegetable oil	5 ml
	salt and pepper	

In a food processor, grind the hazelnuts with the sage leaves until quite fine but not completely powdery. Tip onto a large plate. Trim any excess fat off the pork, and roll in the seasoned flour. Next, coat the floured pork steaks evenly in the beaten egg mixed with the soy milk.

Lastly, roll the pork steaks in the hazelnut and sage mixture. Refrigerate until needed. Pre-heat the oven to 400F.

In a large frying pan, bring the oil to medium heat.

Place the pork in the hot fat, and cook for several minutes until golden brown. Turn over and repeat on other side.

Put the pork steaks in an oven-proof dish, and bake in oven for about 8 minutes.

This could be made with roast of pork, cut into medallions, or for a more economical dish use pork chops.

PER SERVING	
Calories	694
% Calories from fat	71
Fat (g)	56.6
Saturated fat (g)	6.2
Cholesterol (mg)	121.9
Sodium (mg)	68
Protein (g)	37.6
Carbohydrate (g)	15.3
Calcium (mg)	128.5
EXCHANGES	
Milk	0.0
Vegetable	0.0
Fruit	0.0
Bread	1.0
Meat	3.0
Fat	10.0

This could also be done with whole trout. Slash the skin with 3 diagonal cuts on both sides and marinate. Cook under a hot broiler for about 4 minutes on either side so that the skin turns crispy brown.

Try this dish using other fish fillets such as salmon, cod or haddock.

Garam masala is a blend of spices you can find in Indian markets or ethnic food sections.

Fillet of Trout, East Indian Style

Serves 4

For anyone who may find plain fish bland, this dish is interesting in both color and flavor. Serve with Minted Yogurt Sauce on page 116, some brown rice and a salad.

2 tsps	grated fresh gingerroot	2 tsps
2	cloves garlic, crushed	2
1 tsp	salt	1 tsp
1 tsp	ground cumin	1 tsp
1/2 tsp	chili powder	1/2 tsp
1 tsp	ground turmeric	1 tsp
2 tsps	paprika	2 tsps
1 tbsp	sunflower oil	15 ml
2 tbsps	lemon juice	30 ml
2 tbsps	garam masala	2 tbsps
2	big or 4 small trout fillets (12 oz total)	2
1 tbsp	peanut oil	15 ml
1	lemon cut in wedges	1
	watercress to garnish	

Mix all the marinade ingredients together in a bowl.

Spread the marinade over the trout fillets, putting most of the marinade on the skinless side.

Leave in the fridge to marinate for up to 6 hours.

Heat a large non-stick pan with the peanut oil.

Fry the fillets 2–4 minutes on each side until golden and crisp (the time depends on thickness of fillet).

Serve on a warm plate garnished with lemon wedges and watercress.

PER SERVING	
Calories	214
% Calories from fat	54
Fat (g)	13.2
Saturated fat (g)	2
Cholesterol (mg)	49.3
Sodium (mg)	634
Protein (g)	18.9
Carbohydrate (g)	6.6
Calcium (mg)	84.6

EXCHANGES	
Milk	0.0
Vegetable	0.0
Fruit	0.0
Bread	0.0
Meat	3.0
Fat	1.0

Try this sauce with salmon, cod, trout fillet or smoked fish.

If watercress is unavailable, baby spinach leaves make a good alternative.

For a delicious vegetarian dish, serve the sauce with warm new potatoes and hard-boiled eggs.

Grilled Fillet of Trout with Watercress Sauce

Serves 4

This sauce has a lovely creaminess and color that complements grilled fillets of sea trout perfectly. Serve with new potatoes and steamed vegetables. Watercress is a valuable source of vitamins and minerals. It is rich in potassium, calcium and phosphorus, as well as having good quantities of iron, iodine, sodium and magnesium. For this sauce the watercress is hardly cooked at all, which helps retain the nutrients and the color.

1/2 tbsp	mild olive oil or sunflower oil	8 ml
4	trout fillets (about 6 oz each)	4
1 1/4 cups	good fish stock (could use chicken or vegetable bouillon)	300 ml
2 cups	watercress, washed	2 cups
1 cup	(scant) low-fat mayonnaise	1 cup
	salt and freshly ground pepper	
1 tbsp	freshly squeezed lemon juice	15 ml

Lightly oil the fish and lay the fillets on a baking sheet. Pre-heat the broiler.

In a small pan bring the stock to a boil.

Remove the stock from the heat and stir in the watercress. Pour into a processor and blend thoroughly until you have a smooth green liquid.

Pour the sauce back into the pan and gradually whisk in the mayonnaise; it should slightly thicken and have the consistency of cream. Season well with salt and pepper.

Place the fish fillets under hot broiler.

Cook for 4–5 minutes, turn, and cook for 2 minutes until the fish is just cooked through (the cooking time will vary slightly depending on the thickness of the fish fillets).

Arrange the fish fillets on warm serving plates.

Gently warm the sauce, whisking continuously, and gradually add the lemon juice.

Spoon the sauce over the fish fillets and serve.

PER SERVING	
Calories	373
% Calories from fat	41
Fat (g)	16.8
Saturated fat (g)	3
Cholesterol (mg)	110.1
Sodium (mg)	1115
Protein (g)	36.6
Carbohydrate (g)	17.4
Calcium (mg)	138.4

EXCHANGES	
Milk	0.0
Vegetable	0.0
Fruit	0.0
Bread	1.0
Meat	5.5
Fat	0.0

For an alternative, omit the shrimp and use 2 hard-boiled eggs instead.

Fish, Shrimp and Leek Pie

Serves 6

This dish can be prepared in advance and chilled prior to final cooking. It is an impressive and tasty supper for your friends. Serve with new or boiled potatoes and green vegetables.

12 oz	fish fillet (haddock, cod, salmon, etc.)	340 g
	salt and freshly ground pepper	
2 tbsps	vegan margarine	50 g
2	small leeks, finely sliced	2
1 tbsp	all-purpose flour	1 tbsp
²/₃ cup	vegetable stock	150 ml
²/₃ cup	soy milk	150 ml
2 tbsps	chopped parsley	2 tbsps
1 tsp	chopped dill or tarragon	1 tsp
1 tbsp	capers, drained (optional)	1 tbsp
¹/₂ tbsp	lemon juice	8 ml
¹/₂ lb	freshly peeled boiled shrimp or thawed frozen shrimp	225 g
1 lb	puff pastry	450 g
1	egg beaten for the glaze	1

Pre-heat the oven to 425F. Lay the fish in a greased baking dish, season well with salt and pepper, and dot with ¹/₂ oz of the margarine.

Cover with aluminum foil and bake for 15–20 minutes until the fish is just cooked; remove from the oven and allow to cool. Remove the skin and any bones from the fish, and flake into large pieces.

Melt remaining margarine in a saucepan, add the leeks and gently sauté for 10–15 minutes, stirring regularly, until the leeks are tender.

Stir the flour into the leeks and cook for about 2 minutes over medium heat until the flour is cooked but not browned.

Gradually stir the stock and soy milk into the flour, stirring continuously; simmer for about 5 minutes until the sauce becomes thick.

Season with herbs, capers, lemon juice, salt and pepper.

Carefully stir the fish into the sauce, then allow to cool completely. When cool, stir in the shrimp.

PER SERVING	
Calories	587
% Calories from fat	54
Fat (g)	34.9
Saturated fat (g)	8.5
Cholesterol (mg)	141.3
Sodium (mg)	432
Protein (g)	26.8
Carbohydrate (g)	40.9
Calcium (mg)	69.4
EXCHANGES	
Milk	0.0
Vegetable	0.0
Fruit	0.0
Bread	2.5
Meat	3.0
Fat	5.0

On a floured surface, roll the pastry into a 14-inch square.

Lift onto a large oiled baking sheet, and lightly glaze the edge of the pastry with the beaten egg.

Spoon the cold fish and shrimp filling into the center of the pastry.

Pull the opposite corners of the pastry to the center and pinch all the edges together firmly, so you have a square with the pinched edges in the shape of a cross.

Glaze pastry all over with beaten egg.

Bake for 25–30 minutes, until pastry is golden and risen. Serve immediately.

Cajun Blackened Fish

Serves 4

This is a really interesting way of cooking any fish fillet such as haddock, cod or red fish. It is also delicious made with salmon fillet and served with a tangy salsa. Serve with plain basmati rice.

3 tbsps	Cajun spice mix (if you are unable to buy Cajun spice mix, follow the recipe on page 126)	3 tbsps
2 tsps	sweet paprika powder	2 tsps
4	fish fillets (about 7 oz each), skinned	4
1 tbsp	sunflower oil	15 ml
2 oz	vegan margarine	56 g

Mix 2 tablespoons of the Cajun spices with the paprika (remember to save 1 tablespoon of Cajun spice mix for later).

Coat the fish liberally in the spice mix and refrigerate for 6–8 hours. The longer the fish is left coated in the spice mix, the more flavor it will have.

Heat a large non-stick shallow pan over high heat with the oil. Place fillets in hot pan to cook 2 minutes on high heat.

Turn and cook a few minutes longer until it is just cooked through.

Each side of the fish should be well charred. Remove the fish from the pan and keep warm.

In the same pan, melt the margarine, gently so it does not separate, and mix in the remaining tablespoon of Cajun spice mix.

Serve fish on warm plates, and pour the spiced margarine over each fillet.

Choose fish fillets of an even thickness and preferably no more than ³⁄₄ inch thick for best results. This allows the spices to be well absorbed into the fish.

PER SERVING	
Calories	316
% Calories from fat	49
Fat (g)	17
Saturated fat (g)	2.9
Cholesterol (mg)	112.5
Sodium (mg)	270
Protein (g)	37.9
Carbohydrate (g)	1.4
Calcium (mg)	73.3

EXCHANGES	
Milk	0.0
Vegetable	0.0
Fruit	0.0
Bread	0.0
Meat	6.0
Fat	0.0

Tuna is readily available from most supermarkets and fish markets. Provided it is fresh (not previously frozen), it may be stored in your freezer.

Pan-Fried Tuna Steaks with Salsa Verde

Serves 4

This sauce is unusually tangy. It goes extremely well with fresh tuna or swordfish. You can store the salsa in the fridge for several days. Serve this dish with rice or new potatoes.

1 tbsp	olive oil	15 ml
¼ cup	drained cornichons or gherkins (2 oz)	56 g
2 tbsps	drained capers	2 tbsps
	juice from 1 lemon	
	bunch fresh parsley	
	bunch fresh dill	
	bunch fresh cilantro	
4	4-oz tuna steaks, about ¾ inch thick	4
	oil for brushing	
	salt and freshly ground pepper	

Place all the salsa ingredients in a food processor or blender, and blend until just smooth.

Lightly oil a non-stick fry pan, brush tuna with oil and sprinkle with salt and pepper.

When pan is very hot, fry the tuna steaks for about 1 minute. Turn the fish when it has changed to a white color. Cook on the other side for about 30 seconds.

Cook according to personal preference, but I personally like it to be slightly pink in the middle, which keeps the tuna tender.

Transfer to warm plates and spoon a dollop of salsa on each steak.

PER SERVING	
Calories	214
% Calories from fat	39
Fat (g)	9.1
Saturated fat (g)	1.9
Cholesterol (mg)	42.8
Sodium (mg)	280
Protein (g)	27.1
Carbohydrate (g)	5.3
Calcium (mg)	33.9
EXCHANGES	
Milk	0.0
Vegetable	1.0
Fruit	0.0
Bread	0.0
Meat	3.0
Fat	0.0

This dressing would also be suitable served with tilapia.
  If preferred, substitute grated fresh ginger for the horseradish.

Broiled Catfish with Soy, Honey and Horseradish Dressing

Serves 4

The warm dressing adds an oriental touch to the dish. Delicious served with noodles or rice and stir-fry vegetables. Have your fish filleted at the fish market.

4	fillets of catfish, each about 4 oz	4
1 tbsp	olive oil	15 ml
Dressing		
4	green onions	4
2 tbsps	light soy sauce	30 ml
2 tbsps	peanut oil	30 ml
1 tsp	balsamic vinegar	5 ml
2 tsps	fresh grated horseradish	2 tsps
2 tsps	honey	2 tsps

Cut 2 of the green onions into thin julienne strips for garnish. Finely chop the remaining 2.

In a small saucepan, combine the chopped onions, soy sauce, peanut oil, balsamic, horseradish and honey and mix well.

Heat the broiler, place the fillets on a lightly oiled baking sheet, brush the fish with olive oil and season with salt and pepper.

Broil for about 4 minutes either side until the fish is cooked through and golden.

Arrange the fish on a warm platter. Warm the dressing up slightly and spoon over the catfish.

Garnish each fillet with strips of green onion.

PER SERVING	
Calories	264
% Calories from fat	64
Fat (g)	18.7
Saturated fat (g)	3.6
Cholesterol (mg)	52.9
Sodium (mg)	358
Protein (g)	18.4
Carbohydrate (g)	4.9
Calcium (mg)	27.6
EXCHANGES	
Milk	0.0
Vegetable	1.0
Fruit	0.0
Bread	0.0
Meat	2.0
Fat	3.0

Use any white fish fillets.
The uncooked fish fillets topped with the crust may be prepared the day before and stored in the fridge.

Crusted Fillet of Cod

Serves 4

This is a great way to cook plain white fish. We have made this dish at our family restaurants with a herb and fresh Parmesan crust, so I was surprised at how tasty it was made with the soy cheese and mustard powder instead of Parmesan. Serve with the Aioli Sauce (see page 112), new potatoes and green vegetables.

4	cod fillets (about 7–8 oz each)	4
8–10 slices	white bread (about 6 oz)	170 g
½ cup	soy cheese	110 g
1 tsp	mustard powder	1 tsp
1	bunch of parsley	1
	sprig of fresh dill	
	sprig of fresh basil	
2 tbsps	olive oil	30 ml
	salt and freshly ground pepper	

Pre-heat the oven to 375F. Lay the fish fillets skin side down on a large greased baking sheet.

In a food processor, process the bread, soy cheese, mustard powder and herbs until well crumbed.

Stir in the olive oil and season well. Press the mixture on the top of the fish fillets so it lies evenly about ¼ inch thick.

Roast in the oven for 15–20 minutes until the crust is golden and the fish is cooked through.

Serve on warm plates.

PER SERVING	
Calories	485
% Calories from fat	42
Fat (g)	22.4
Saturated fat (g)	3.8
Cholesterol (mg)	85.1
Sodium (mg)	551
Protein (g)	42.1
Carbohydrate (g)	27.2
Calcium (mg)	108.7

EXCHANGES	
Milk	0.0
Vegetable	0.0
Fruit	0.0
Bread	2.0
Meat	5.0
Fat	1.5

If using wooden skewers, soak them in hot water for several minutes before threading the food onto them. This helps prevent charring during cooking.

The brochettes would be equally delicious made using salmon or swordfish.

Monkfish and Shrimp Brochettes

Serves 4

Monkfish is an ideal fish for brochettes, as it has a slightly meaty texture and holds its shape well. These would be perfect for a barbecue or a smart dinner party dish. They could be served with plain basmati rice, which looks quite stylish put into a ramekin and turned out onto each plate as a timbale shape.

1lb 4oz	fresh monkfish tail	560 g
16	large shrimp, uncooked, either in or out of shell	16
4	wooden or metal skewers	4
	Lime and Cilantro Dressing (see page 142)	

Prepare monkfish: skin, fillet and cut into 1-inch cubes (aim for 16–20 cubes in total).

Push alternate cubes of monkfish and shrimp onto the 4 skewers. Cover and leave in the fridge until required. Pre-heat the broiler. Place the kebabs on a suitable baking dish for broiling.

Brush the kebabs with the dressing. Cook under hot broiler 5–8 minutes. Turn and repeat until the fish becomes slightly golden in color. Baste occasionally with the dressing. Serve on warm plates.

Pour any juices from the oven dish over the brochettes.

Warm the remaining dressing in a small saucepan and spoon some of it over each brochette, ensuring that each person gets plenty of chili, ginger and cilantro mixture.

Garnish with chopped cilantro leaves.

PER SERVING	
Calories	336
% Calories from fat	61
Fat (g)	22.8
Saturated fat (g)	4
Cholesterol (mg)	77.1
Sodium (mg)	416
Protein (g)	26.8
Carbohydrate (g)	5.9
Calcium (mg)	32.2

EXCHANGES	
Milk	0.0
Vegetable	0.0
Fruit	0.0
Bread	0.0
Meat	4.0
Fat	2.5

Mahi-mahi should be bought very fresh. Make sure the fish you choose is bright, rigid and shiny, not dull and tired looking.

Crunchy Oat-Coated Mahi-Mahi Fillets

Serves 4

For this dish the fillets are cooked in crunchy oatmeal, making them more appealing to those who may not be fish lovers but who know the benefits of eating fresh fish.

4	mahi-mahi fillets, about 4–6 oz each	4
1/4 cup	soy milk	60 ml
1/4 cup	oatmeal, uncooked	1/4 cup
2 tbsps	olive oil	30 ml
1	large lemon, cut into wedges	1

Remove any small bones from the fillets.

Dip each fillet in the soy milk, then roll it liberally in the oatmeal.

Heat a large frying pan with the oil.

When hot, fry the fillets for 2–3 minutes on either side until crisp and golden and just cooked through.

Serve on a warm plate with wedges of lemon.

PER SERVING	
Calories	185
% Calories from fat	39
Fat (g)	8.2
Saturated fat (g)	1.2
Cholesterol (mg)	82.5
Sodium (mg)	103
Protein (g)	22.5
Carbohydrate (g)	6.6
Calcium (mg)	36.7
EXCHANGES	
Milk	0.0
Vegetable	0.0
Fruit	0.0
Bread	0.5
Meat	3.0
Fat	0.0

For a delicious vegan dish, try using parsnips instead of haddock and potatoes. Garam masala, an Indian blend of spices, may be found in ethnic sections or Indian grocery stores.

Potato-Crusted Haddock and Curried Tomato Bake

Serves 4

Serve as a complete meal, maybe with a few salad leaves or baby spinach. The bake can be made a day in advance and kept in the fridge before cooking. The addition of coconut milk gives the dish a delicious buttery flavor.

4–6	potatoes (about 1¹/₂ lb)	675 g
2 tbsps	olive oil	30 ml
1	medium onion, finely chopped	1
1 tbsp	chopped fresh gingerroot	1 tbsp
2	cloves garlic, crushed	2
1 tsp	garam masala	1 tsp
1 tsp	ground turmeric	1 tsp
2 tsps	ground cumin	2 tsps
1 tsp	ground cilantro	1 tsp
6	tomatoes (about 1 lb), chopped coarsely (or use one 14-oz can of chopped tomatoes)	6
1 tsp	vegan bouillon powder	1 tsp
2 tbsps	chopped fresh cilantro leaves	2 tbsps
4	small fillets or 2 large fillets fresh haddock, skinned, about 6–7 oz per person	4
²/₃ cup	reduced-fat coconut milk	150 ml
	salt and freshly ground pepper	

Pre-heat the oven to 375F. Peel and slice the potatoes about ¹/₄ inch thick.

Boil or steam the potatoes for 8–10 minutes until half cooked; allow to cool.

Heat 1 tablespoon of the olive oil in a medium pan, and sauté the onion, ginger and garlic for about 5 minutes until soft. Stir in the ground spices and cook, stirring well, for about 2 minutes.

Add the tomatoes and bouillon powder and stir over the heat for 5–10 minutes or until tomato is tender; stir in the fresh cilantro and season well.

Layer half the potatoes in a large, greased baking dish.

Cut the fish fillets into quarters and lay them over the potatoes. Spoon the tomato sauce over the fish, covering well.

PER SERVING	
Calories	433
% Calories from fat	23
Fat (g)	10.9
Saturated fat (g)	2.5
Cholesterol (mg)	96.4
Sodium (mg)	391
Protein (g)	39.7
Carbohydrate (g)	44.6
Calcium (mg)	116
EXCHANGES	
Milk	0.0
Vegetable	0.0
Fruit	0.0
Bread	3.0
Meat	4.0
Fat	0.0

Top with the remaining potatoes, pour over the coconut milk and drizzle with 1 tablespoon olive oil. Season with salt and freshly ground pepper.

Bake for about 25 minutes until cooked through.

Broil the top if necessary for a golden potato crust.

You could also use smoked herring fillets in this recipe. As they have many small pin bones, I suggest you process the herring in a food processor first. The dish would contain plenty of calcium, as the bones will have been ground up.

Smoked Fish Cakes

Serves 4 (2 cakes per serving)

These fish cakes make a pleasant change from the cod and salmon variety you can buy from supermarkets. I recommend that you serve them with the Tangy Mayonnaise on page 120 and a crisp salad.

6–8	potatoes (about 1 lb)	450 g
1 lb	mixed fish fillets (such as smoked haddock, smoked salmon, tilapia, white fish)	450 g
3	green onions, washed, cut into thin rings	3
1	large egg, beaten	1
2 tsps	capers, drained	2 tsps
2 tbsps	chopped parsley	2 tbsps
1 tbsp	lemon juice	15 ml
1 tsp	anchovy paste	1 tsp
	freshly ground pepper	

Coating

1½ tbsps	all-purpose flour seasoned with salt and pepper	1½ tbsps
1	egg, beaten	1
1 tbsp	soy milk	15 ml
²/₃ cup	breadcrumbs	150 g
	vegetable oil for pan-frying the fish cakes	
	lemon wedges to garnish	

Pre-heat the oven to 350F. Peel and chop the potatoes. Boil until soft, then mash well.

Place the fish (except those smoked, which have already been cooked) on a greased baking sheet, cover with aluminum foil and

PER SERVING	
Calories	361
% Calories from fat	12
Fat (g)	5
Saturated fat (g)	1.2
Cholesterol (mg)	194
Sodium (mg)	1126
Protein (g)	38.7
Carbohydrate (g)	39.4
Calcium (mg)	142.9
EXCHANGES	
Milk	0.0
Vegetable	0.0
Fruit	0.0
Bread	2.5
Meat	4.0
Fat	0.0

bake for about 20 minutes, until the fish is just cooked. Allow to cool slightly.

Flake the fish into a large bowl, discarding any skin and bones.

In a large bowl, mix together the mashed potato, the flaked fish and all the remaining fish cake ingredients and seasonings; mix thoroughly.

Divide the mixture into 8 equal balls, flatten out and pat into a neat shape.

Dip each fish cake into the flour, then the beaten egg mixed with soy milk, then the breadcrumbs.

Pan-fry the fish cakes in a small amount of vegetable oil for about 3 minutes on either side over medium heat until golden brown.

Then transfer the fish cakes to the oven and cook for 10–15 minutes to ensure they're well heated throughout and crisp on the outside.

Serve with lemon wedges.

If you prefer, use smoked salmon fillet. Be sure to remove all the pin bones before covering with rarebit topping.

Smoked Trout Rarebit

Serves 4

Smoked fish goes very well with a tomatoes-and-cheese-style topping. For anyone missing the flavor of real cheese, this tastes quite convincingly cheesy! Delicious served with rice or potatoes.

4	smoked trout fillets (6–7 oz each), skinned and cut in half	4
4	large tomatoes	4
1	egg	1
1	egg yolk	1
2 tbsps	Dijon mustard	2 tbsps
3/8 cup	soy cheese	80 g
1 tsp	Worcestershire sauce	1 tsp
	salt, freshly ground pepper and a pinch of cayenne	
1 tbsp	freshly chopped parsley	1 tbsp
	watercress to garnish	

PER SERVING	
Calories	392
% Calories from fat	40
Fat (g)	17
Saturated fat (g)	3.5
Cholesterol (mg)	237.3
Sodium (mg)	1678
Protein (g)	48.6
Carbohydrate (g)	8.3
Calcium (mg)	118.8

EXCHANGES	
Milk	0.0
Vegetable	0.0
Fruit	0.0
Bread	0.0
Meat	7.0
Fat	0.0

Pre-heat the oven to 350F. Lay the fillets in a large greased baking dish, keeping them separate.

Cut each tomato into six discs. Cover the fillets with a layer of sliced tomatoes.

Beat together all the remaining ingredients. Spread over the tomatoes to form an even layer.

Bake for 20–25 minutes or until golden and slightly risen.

Place each fillet onto a warm plate garnished with sprigs of watercress.

Split Pea and Vegetable Pot Pie

Serves 6

This pot pie is a vegetable bake with a savory scone topping. It is a hearty, filling meal and extremely economical. This version uses yellow split peas, giving an interesting texture. The addition of soy flour makes the scones more nutritious, and along with the yeast extract and mustard powder, gives them a savory cheese taste. Serve with some leafy vegetables. Any leftover is great reheated.

Split pea and vegetable base

1/2 cup	dry yellow split peas (3 1/2 oz), soaked in cold water for 10 minutes	98 g
1	large onion, finely chopped	1
1 tbsp	olive oil	15 ml
1	leek, finely chopped	1
2	ribs celery, finely chopped	2
3	cloves garlic, crushed	3
2	medium carrots, peeled and diced	2
1	14-oz can chopped tomatoes	1
2 tbsps	tomato purée	2 tbsps
3/4 cup	vegetable stock (or use vegan bouillon powder)	180 ml
1/2 cup	stringbeans, top and tailed and cut into quarters lengthways (4 oz)	112 g
1	large sprig fresh thyme	1
1 tbsp	freshly chopped parsley	1 tbsp
	salt and freshly ground pepper	

This dish is equally nice with other types of beans or lentils. Instead of the split peas, aduki beans are particularly good.

The scones could be baked separately as savory "cheese-style" scones.

VEGAN

PER SERVING

Calories	229
% Calories from fat	28
Fat (g)	7.4
Saturated fat (g)	1.2
Cholesterol (mg)	0
Sodium (mg)	530
Protein (g)	9.1
Carbohydrate (g)	33.2
Calcium (mg)	110

EXCHANGES

Milk	0.0
Vegetable	0.0
Fruit	0.0
Bread	2.0
Meat	1.0
Fat	1.0

Scone topping

3/4 cup	self-rising flour	3/4 cup
2 tbsps	soy flour (use whole wheat flour if preferred)	2 tbsps
1 tsp	mustard powder	1 tsp
2 tbsps	vegan margarine	50 g
1 tsp	yeast extract (Marmite)	1 tsp
1/2 cup	cold water	120 ml
	soy milk for brushing	

Pre-heat the oven to 400F. Drain the yellow split peas, then tip into a small saucepan covered with cold water, bring to a boil and simmer for 20–25 minutes until just tender (not over-cooked, as they will be cooked further).

In a separate large saucepan, over medium heat sauté the onion in the olive oil.

After a couple of minutes, add the leek, celery, garlic and carrots, and continue cooking for about 8 minutes.

Add the chopped tomatoes, purée, stock and stringbeans. Continue cooking until the vegetables are just tender but still slightly crisp (5–10 minutes).

Mix in the split peas and herbs, and season well.

Pour into a large oven-proof dish (preferably shallow; if the dish is too deep the mixture will not heat through in time). Smooth down and set to one side while you make the scone topping.

Mix the flours and mustard powder, and rub in the margarine until it resembles breadcrumbs.

Stir the yeast extract into the water until dissolved.

Using a knife, pour the water into the flour mixture and blend until it forms dough. Knead lightly in extra flour.

Roll out to about 1/2 inch thick and, using a 1 1/2- or 2-inch fluted or plain pastry cutter, cut out about 12 scones (allowing for 2 scones per serving).

Place the scones on top of the vegetable mixture, and brush with a little soy milk.

Bake in pre-heated oven for 15–20 minutes, until scones are golden and risen.

To serve, spoon onto individual plates with 2 scones arranged on top.

If you are unable to find all these mushrooms, don't worry. Ordinary mushrooms will be fine, although not as exotic.

Individual Mushroom and Walnut Strudels

Serves 4

These tasty strudels can be made in advance and cooked when required. Serve with a crisp dressed salad and perhaps Roasted Tomato Sauce (see page 119).

3–4 slices	stale bread (about 4 oz)	112 g
3	cloves garlic, peeled	3
	bunch of fresh parsley	
2 tbsps	olive oil	30 ml
1	onion, chopped	1
1	small leek, chopped	1
1/2 lb	mixed mushrooms, such as oyster shiitake, morel, flat and wild	225 g
2 tbsps	soy flour	2 tbsps
1 tbsp	soy sauce	15 ml
1 tsp	vegan vegetable bouillon powder	1 tsp
1 tsp	chopped fresh tarragon	1 tsp
2 tbsps	roughly chopped walnut pieces (2 oz)	56 g
	freshly ground pepper	
2 tbsps	vegan margarine	50 g
4	sheets of filo pastry, each measuring about 18 x 12 inches	4
	sesame seeds to sprinkle	

Pre-heat the oven to 400F. Place the bread, garlic and parsley in a food processor and process for about 30 seconds or until finely crumbed; tip this breadcrumb mixture into a bowl.

Heat the olive oil in a large pan and sauté the onion and leek over medium heat for about 5 minutes.

If using shiitake and morel mushrooms, chop finely; roughly chop flat, oyster or wild mushrooms.

Add the chopped mushrooms to the onions and cook for a further 5 minutes.

Mix in the soy flour, soy sauce, bouillon, tarragon and walnuts, and fry gently for a further minute. Season with pepper; you may not need to add salt. Allow to cool.

VEGAN

PER SERVING	
Calories	317
% Calories from fat	50
Fat (g)	17.8
Saturated fat (g)	2.8
Cholesterol (mg)	0.3
Sodium (mg)	824
Protein (g)	7
Carbohydrate (g)	33.5
Calcium (mg)	79.4

EXCHANGES	
Milk	0.0
Vegetable	0.0
Fruit	0.0
Bread	2.0
Meat	0.0
Fat	3.5

Melt the margarine in a small saucepan.

Lay out a single sheet of filo pastry on floured surface, shortest side at the front, and brush the sheet with the margarine.

Sprinkle with a handful of the breadcrumb mixture, covering the entire sheet.

Spoon one-quarter of the mushroom mixture at the front of the rectangle, leaving about 3 inches at either end.

Begin to roll up. After one rotation, brush the ends and fold them in 3 inches from either side; brush dry sides and roll up into sausage. The mixture should be completely contained in the filo pastry.

Repeat for the remaining strudels, and arrange all 4 on a greased baking sheet. Brush with margarine and sprinkle with sesame seeds.

Bake for 15–20 minutes or until pastry is crisp and golden.

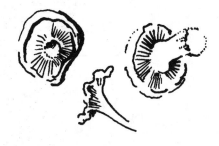

Vegetables

Cumin-Spiced Cauliflower
Stringbeans à la Greque
Stir-Fried Cabbage and Carrots with Caraway
Piquant Vegetables
Fava Beans with Smoked Bacon
Roasted Parsnips with Sesame and Honey
Potato and Celeriac Boulangère
Wholegrain Mustard Mashed Potatoes
Roasted Garlic Mashed Potatoes
Spicy Potato Wedges
Pan-Fried "Cheese" Polenta
Sesame Noodles
Sicilian Caponata
Spiced Rice
Yorkshire Puddings

Try this dish with broccoli instead.

Cumin-Spiced Cauliflower

Serves 6

This is an interesting way to cook cauliflower; delicious with rice and other Indian dishes or as a quick light supper with naan bread.

1	large cauliflower	1
1 tbsp	peanut oil	15 ml
1 tsp	cumin seeds	1 tsp
1 tsp	black mustard seeds	1 tsp
1 tsp	ground cumin	1 tsp
1 tsp	ground cilantro	1 tsp
1/2 tsp	ground turmeric	1/2 tsp
2/3 cup	vegetable stock	150 ml

Break cauliflower into florets, keeping as much stalk as possible. Cut the bigger florets if necessary.

Heat oil in a large wok or frying pan. When hot add cumin seeds and mustard seeds.

Cook for 1 minute stirring continuously, without burning.

Add ground cumin, cilantro and turmeric, and cook for 1 further minute.

Add cauliflower and toss the florets in the spices. Pour in the vegetable stock and mix thoroughly.

Cover and simmer for about 5 minutes over medium heat until the cauliflower is cooked but still firm.

Serve immediately.

PER SERVING

Calories	56
% Calories from fat	43
Fat (g)	3
Saturated fat (g)	0.4
Cholesterol (mg)	0
Sodium (mg)	106
Protein (g)	3.7
Carbohydrate (g)	5.4
Calcium (mg)	44.1

EXCHANGES

Milk	0.0
Vegetable	1.0
Fruit	0.0
Bread	0.0
Meat	0.0
Fat	0.5

You can also use okra for this dish, as it contains large amounts of calcium.

This dish is good to freeze, and it is also a great way of using up zucchini.

Stringbeans à la Greque

Serves 4–6

This has to be one of the nicest ways of cooking stringbeans. In the summer my parents are always giving me buckets full of home-grown beans. I usually cook a large batch of this recipe and eat them either hot with a baked potato or cold as part of a salad. This dish seems to improve when reheated the following day.

2 tbsps	olive oil	30 ml
2	cloves garlic, crushed	2
3–4 cups	stringbeans, tops and tails removed (12 oz)	340 g
1 cup	vegetable stock	240 ml
1/2 cup	tomato purée	1/2 cup
1 tsp	sugar	8 g
	salt and freshly ground pepper	

Heat olive oil in a medium saucepan. Add garlic and stringbeans and stir over medium heat for 2 minutes.

Add stock and tomato purée and stir well.

Simmer over low heat, stirring occasionally, for 15–20 minutes until sauce has reduced slightly and thickened and the beans are just cooked.

Season with sugar, salt and pepper before serving.

PER SERVING	
Calories	115
% Calories from fat	53
Fat (g)	7.3
Saturated fat (g)	0.9
Cholesterol (mg)	0
Sodium (mg)	179
Protein (g)	2.7
Carbohydrate (g)	11.8
Calcium (mg)	51.1

EXCHANGES	
Milk	0.0
Vegetable	2.0
Fruit	0.0
Bread	0.0
Meat	0.0
Fat	1.5

Use other vegetable combinations, such as zucchini, red cabbage, Chinese cabbage, etc.

You may omit the caraway seeds for children. If you don't like caraway, black mustard seeds are also a good combination with cabbage.

Stir-Fried Cabbage and Carrots with Caraway

Serves 4

This is an ideal way of cooking vegetables to retain the maximum amount of water-soluble vitamins, and the addition of stock gives the stir-fry more flavor. To make more of a meal, add chopped bacon to the vegetables and serve with Spicy Potato Wedges (see page 105).

1 lb	white cabbage	450 g
1–2	medium carrots (½ lb)	225 g
2 tbsps	olive oil, or walnut oil	30 ml
⅔ cup	vegetable or chicken stock	150 ml
1 tsp	caraway seeds	1 tsp
	salt and freshly ground pepper	

Shred the cabbage finely. Peel the carrots and either cut into thin julienne strips or use a vegetable peeler to make ribbons. Heat a large wok or frying pan, heat the oil until hot and throw in the cabbage and carrots.

Stir-fry for several minutes, then add the stock, caraway seeds and seasonings.

Continue frying for a further 3 or 4 minutes until the cabbage is cooked but still slightly crisp.

Serve in a warm dish.

PER SERVING	
Calories	108
% Calories from fat	57
Fat (g)	7.3
Saturated fat (g)	1
Cholesterol (mg)	0
Sodium (mg)	177
Protein (g)	2.7
Carbohydrate (g)	9.7
Calcium (mg)	141.3
EXCHANGES	
Milk	0.0
Vegetable	2.0
Fruit	0.0
Bread	0.0
Meat	0.0
Fat	1.5

Suitable for freezing. Otherwise it lasts well for several days in the fridge.

Piquant Vegetables

Serves 4

I discovered this dish while experimenting with Cajun cooking. It makes a delicious accompaniment to Cajun-style fish or chicken.

1	medium onion	1
1	medium green bell pepper	1
1	small red chili pepper	1
3	ribs celery	3
1 tsp	vegetable oil	5 ml
2	cloves garlic, crushed	2
1 tsp	paprika	1 tsp
1 tsp	Cajun spice mix (either bought or the homemade recipe on page 126)	1 tsp
1	14-oz can chopped tomatoes	1
1/4 tsp	Tabasco	1/4 tsp
1 cup	water	240 ml
1/2 tsp	dried oregano	1/2 tsp
1 tsp	sugar	8 g
	salt and freshly ground pepper	

Finely chop onion, peppers and celery.

Heat a large frying pan with the oil, and sauté the vegetables and garlic for about 5 minutes.

Stir in the spices and cook for 1 minute; then mix in the tomatoes, Tabasco, water, oregano and sugar and simmer uncovered for about 12 minutes.

Season with salt and pepper before serving.

PER SERVING	
Calories	67
% Calories from fat	21
Fat (g)	1.8
Saturated fat (g)	0.2
Cholesterol (mg)	0
Sodium (mg)	355
Protein (g)	2.7
Carbohydrate (g)	12.1
Calcium (mg)	39.9

EXCHANGES	
Milk	0.0
Vegetable	2.0
Fruit	0.0
Bread	0.0
Meat	0.0
Fat	0.0

The season for fava beans is fairly short, although you could use beans defrosted from frozen, which are available throughout the year. Also try with other beans such as cooked kidney, cannellini or butter beans.

Fava Beans with Smoked Bacon

Serves 4

Delicious as a vegetable accompaniment or as a quick supper dish with rice, pasta or potatoes.

2 lb	fava beans	900 g
2 tbsps	olive oil	30 ml
1	large red onion, cut in half and thinly sliced	1
6–8 slices	bacon (about 6 oz)	170 g
2	cloves garlic, crushed	2
½ tbsp	sherry vinegar	8 ml
1 tbsp	chopped parsley	1 tbsp
	salt and freshly ground pepper	

Remove the beans from the pods. Steam or boil for 5–8 minutes until just tender.

Remove the rind from the bacon and cut into strips.

Meanwhile, in large frying pan, heat 1 tablespoon olive oil, and sauté the onion for about 5 minutes.

Add the bacon and garlic and cook for a further 8–10 minutes over medium heat, until beginning to caramelize and turn golden at the edges. Toss in the sherry vinegar and cook for a further minute.

Tip the beans into the mixture and heat through for several minutes.

Remove from heat; add remaining olive oil, parsley, salt and pepper.

PER SERVING	
Calories	511
% Calories from fat	48
Fat (g)	29.4
Saturated fat (g)	8.6
Cholesterol (mg)	36.1
Sodium (mg)	735
Protein (g)	30.8
Carbohydrate (g)	41.9
Calcium (mg)	96

EXCHANGES	
Milk	0.0
Vegetable	0.0
Fruit	0.0
Bread	3.0
Meat	0.0
Fat	6.0

Try a combination of root vegetables such as carrots, beets, sweet potatoes, etc.

Roasted Parsnips with Sesame and Honey

Serves 4

This jazzes up your Sunday roast and might make parsnips more appealing to children.

4	medium parsnips (1 lb)	450 g
1 tbsp	vegetable oil	15 ml
	salt and freshly ground pepper	
1 tbsp	sesame oil	15 ml
1½ tsps	honey	1½ tsps
2 tsps	sesame seeds	2 tsps

Pre-heat the oven to 400F. Peel and cut parsnips into about 3-inch-long by 1-inch-thick sticks.

In a large baking dish, mix the parsnips with the vegetable oil, salt and pepper.

Roast for about 30 minutes, turning once or twice.

When the parsnips are cooked through, golden and slightly crisp, remove from oven.

Mix sesame oil and honey together.

Toss the parsnips with the oil and honey mixture until completely covered.

Sprinkle over sesame seeds. Return to oven and cook for a further 10 minutes.

Serve immediately.

PER SERVING	
Calories	168
% Calories from fat	40
Fat (g)	7.9
Saturated fat (g)	1.1
Cholesterol (mg)	0
Sodium (mg)	12
Protein (g)	1.9
Carbohydrate (g)	24.4
Calcium (mg)	43.9

EXCHANGES	
Milk	0.0
Vegetable	0.0
Fruit	0.0
Bread	1.5
Meat	0.0
Fat	1.5

Try with parsnips instead of the celeriac.

Potato and Celeriac Boulangère

Serves 4

This combination is a winner. It is a great low-fat vegetable accompaniment, with the stock preventing the dish from becoming dry.

5–6	small potatoes (about 7/8 lb)	400 g
5/8 lb	celeriac (10 oz)	280 g
1	onion, sliced	1
1 1/2 cups	chicken or vegetable stock	360 ml
1 tbsp	olive oil	15 ml
	salt and freshly ground pepper	

Pre-heat the oven to 350F. Peel potatoes and celeriac. Cut into thin slices. Lay alternating slices of celeriac and potato with the onion in a shallow, greased roasting pan, making sure the onion is not on the top.

Season the stock with salt and pepper. Pour the stock over the potatoes and celeriac, and brush the top with the olive oil, drizzling the remainder over.

Bake uncovered for about 1 hour until lightly browned on top. To test if the vegetables are cooked, push a metal skewer or sharp knife into the dish; it should feel soft.

If after about 40 minutes, the top is burning but it is not cooked, cover with foil and continue cooking. When done, serve immediately.

PER SERVING	
Calories	178
% Calories from fat	21
Fat (g)	4.4
Saturated fat (g)	0.5
Cholesterol (mg)	9.4
Sodium (mg)	165
Protein (g)	7.4
Carbohydrate (g)	28.7
Calcium (mg)	54.9

EXCHANGES	
Milk	0.0
Vegetable	0.0
Fruit	0.0
Bread	2.0
Meat	0.0
Fat	1.0

Wholegrain Mustard Mashed Potatoes

Serves 4

Delicious with pork or liver, or as a topping for savory pies such as the Smoked Ham and Lentil Pie (see page 42).

6–8	small potatoes (about 1 1/2 lb)	675 g
1 tbsp	vegan margarine	25 g
2 tbsps	soy cream	30 ml
1 tbsp	wholegrain mustard	1 tbsp
	salt and freshly ground pepper	

Peel and cut potatoes into halves or quarters depending on size.

Steam or boil the potatoes until they are cooked through and fairly soft; drain.

In a large pan, gently melt margarine with soy cream, then remove from the heat.

Tip in the potatoes, and mash well until completely smooth.

Stir in mustard and seasonings. Serve hot.

PER SERVING	
Calories	191
% Calories from fat	17
Fat (g)	3.7
Saturated fat (g)	0.6
Cholesterol (mg)	0
Sodium (mg)	96
Protein (g)	5.8
Carbohydrate (g)	34.3
Calcium (mg)	33.3

EXCHANGES	
Milk	0.0
Vegetable	0.0
Fruit	0.0
Bread	2.5
Meat	0.0
Fat	0.5

Try using sweet potatoes or parsnips for a more exotic touch.

Roasted Garlic Mashed Potatoes

Serves 4–6

This is a great way of making mashed potatoes without butter and cream; it is also a lot more nutritious. Don't worry, once the garlic is roasted it is not as potent as a whole bulb of raw garlic might seem, and think how healthy it is. Delicious served with meats, fish or just about anything.

1	bulb of garlic, whole	1
6–8	small potatoes (about 1 1/2 lb)	675 g
3 tbsps	olive oil	45 ml
1 tsp	salt	1 tsp
	freshly ground pepper to taste	

Pre-heat the oven to 400F. Slice approximately 1/2 inch off the top stalk-end of the garlic so as to just reveal each clove.

Roast garlic in the oven for 20–25 minutes until soft and golden, not dark brown.

Meanwhile, peel the potatoes and either steam or boil them until cooked. Don't worry if they are slightly overcooked, as this makes for a wetter mashed potato.

When garlic is cool enough to handle, peel off skin and pop out the whole garlic cloves, which should be soft.

In a bowl, mash the garlic, olive oil and salt to form a paste.

Add the garlic paste to the mashed potatoes and more olive oil if they seem dry, then season with freshly ground pepper.

Heat through gently before serving.

PER SERVING	
Calories	257
% Calories from fat	35
Fat (g)	10.5
Saturated fat (g)	1.4
Cholesterol (mg)	0
Sodium (mg)	583
Protein (g)	6.3
Carbohydrate (g)	36.7
Calcium (mg)	48.9
EXCHANGES	
Milk	0.0
Vegetable	0.0
Fruit	0.0
Bread	2.5
Meat	0.0
Fat	2.0

A great way to use up any leftover new potatoes.

Spicy Potato Wedges

Serves 4

Perfect as an accompaniment to pork and lamb dishes. The addition of Cajun spices makes the potatoes rather special. Even my children love these, despite the slightly spicy kick.

4–6	new potatoes (about 1 lb), washed but unpeeled	450 g
2 tsps	Cajun spice mix, bought (or see page 126)	2 tsps
1 tsp	paprika	1 tsp
1 tsp	salt	1 tsp
1	clove garlic, crushed	1
1 tbsp	olive oil	15 ml

Pre-heat the oven to 400F. Boil the potatoes until nearly cooked.

Leaving skins on the potatoes, cut them into quarters lengthways.

Place potatoes in a roasting dish and cover them evenly with the spices, salt, crushed garlic and olive oil until well coated.

Bake in the oven for about 20 minutes until cooked through, crisp and golden brown. Serve hot.

PER SERVING	
Calories	138
% Calories from fat	23
Fat (g)	3.7
Saturated fat (g)	0.5
Cholesterol (mg)	0
Sodium (mg)	815
Protein (g)	4
Carbohydrate (g)	23.7
Calcium (mg)	28.6

EXCHANGES	
Milk	0.0
Vegetable	0.0
Fruit	0.0
Bread	1.5
Meat	0.0
Fat	0.5

Suitable for a gluten-free diet. Make ahead and store for up to 2 days in the fridge.

Pan-Fried "Cheese" Polenta

Serves 4

Delicious served with Italian dishes such as Sicilian Caponata (see page 108). Usually this is made with strong cheddar, but with the addition of mustard, soy flour and yeast extract, a cheese flavor is achieved.

2½ cups	water	600 ml
½ cup	easy cook, fine polenta (4 oz)	112 g
2 tbsps	soy flour	2 tbsps
2 tsps	French mustard	2 tsps
1 tsp	yeast extract (Marmite)	1 tsp
	salt and freshly ground pepper	
1–2 tbsps	olive oil	15–30 ml

Bring the water to a boil in a medium-size pan. When the water is at a rolling boil, add the polenta, beating the mixture vigorously to stop lumps from forming.

Simmer for about 10 minutes, stirring occasionally.

Continue beating and add the soy flour, mustard, yeast extract and seasonings.

Continue cooking over medium heat for several minutes.

Pour into an 8-inch greased ceramic dish and smooth down flat.

Refrigerate for about 2 hours until set. When cool, cut into quarters.

Heat the olive oil in a large non-stick frying pan. Place the polenta slices in the frying pan.

Cook over medium heat for about 8 minutes each side.

The polenta is ready to serve when it is golden brown on either side.

PER SERVING	
Calories	104
% Calories from fat	36
Fat (g)	4.2
Saturated fat (g)	0.5
Cholesterol (mg)	0
Sodium (mg)	137
Protein (g)	2.8
Carbohydrate (g)	13.6
Calcium (mg)	6.7

EXCHANGES	
Milk	0.0
Vegetable	0.0
Fruit	0.0
Bread	1.0
Meat	0.0
Fat	1.0

For a complete meal, stir-fry vegetables and strips of chicken or pork and add this to the noodles.

Sesame Noodles

Serves 6

Suitable as an accompaniment to Chinese meat dishes and stir-fry vegetables.

1	12-oz pkg medium egg noodles	340 g
2 tbsps	sesame oil	30 ml
2 tbsps	sesame seeds	2 tbsps
5	green onions, finely chopped	5

Bring a large pan of water up to a rolling boil. Add the noodles and make sure they are fully covered in water.

Boil for about 4 minutes (or until just cooked). Strain the noodles.

Pour sesame oil into the pan, add sesame seeds and green onions, and stir over medium heat for several minutes to heat through.

Return the noodles to the pan and stir thoroughly. Serve immediately.

PER SERVING	
Calories	276
% Calories from fat	27
Fat (g)	8.4
Saturated fat (g)	1.4
Cholesterol (mg)	54
Sodium (mg)	9
Protein (g)	8.9
Carbohydrate (g)	41.6
Calcium (mg)	29.2
EXCHANGES	
Milk	0.0
Vegetable	0.0
Fruit	0.0
Bread	3.0
Meat	0.0
Fat	1.5

Sicilian Caponata

Serves 4

This is a sweet-and-sour type of ratatouille. It can be served hot, at room temperature or cold. Leaving it to stand allows the flavors to develop. Delicious with Italian bread such as the foccacia on page 173 for a light meal. Alternatively, serve with rice, polenta or pasta.

2 tbsps	olive oil	30 ml
1	red onion, chopped	1
3	cloves garlic, crushed	3
1	red chili pepper, de-seeded and finely chopped	1
1	red bell pepper, de-seeded and cut in long strips	1
1	yellow bell pepper, de-seeded and cut in long strips	1
1	large eggplant, cut in 1-inch strips	1
1	14-oz can chopped tomatoes	1
1 tbsp	tomato purée	1 tbsp
²/₃ cup	vegetable stock	150 ml
1 tbsp	white wine vinegar	15 ml
1 tbsp	sugar	25 g
15	pitted olives, sliced	15
1 tbsp	drained capers	1 tbsp
	salt and freshly ground pepper	
2 tbsps	chopped fresh basil	2 tbsps

In large pan, heat 1 tablespoon of olive oil, and fry onion and garlic for about 2 minutes.

Add chili pepper, bell peppers and eggplant, and stir well for about 4 minutes.

Add canned tomatoes, purée, stock, vinegar and sugar, and simmer for about 25 minutes or until eggplant and peppers are tender.

Add olives and capers, and season well.

Just before serving, mix in fresh chopped basil and the remaining tablespoon of olive oil.

PER SERVING	
Calories	195
% Calories from fat	41
Fat (g)	9.6
Saturated fat (g)	1.2
Cholesterol (mg)	0
Sodium (mg)	513
Protein (g)	4.8
Carbohydrate (g)	26.4
Calcium (mg)	60.3

EXCHANGES	
Milk	0.0
Vegetable	5.0
Fruit	0.0
Bread	0.0
Meat	0.0
Fat	1.5

Take care not to overcook basmati rice, as it goes very mushy. Brown long-grain rice is also very good cooked this way.

The spiced rice reheats well at a later date either covered with plastic wrap and microwaved or covered with foil and baked in the oven.

Garam masala is an Indian spice that may be found in ethnic aisles or at Indian grocery stores.

Spiced Rice

Serves 4–6

This rice dish has been one of my family's favorites for a long time. After making the spiced onion mixture it will taste surprisingly strong before the rice is added, but don't be alarmed. Once the rice has been added the taste will be much more subtle. I often serve this dish with barbecues, with a tomato relish and lamb kebabs, accompanied by a cucumber and yogurt salad.

1½ cups	basmati rice	330 g
2 tbsps	sunflower oil	30 ml
2	medium onions, very finely chopped	2
3 tsps	ground cumin	3 tsps
1 tsp	curry powder	1 tsp
2 tsps	garam masala	2 tsps
½ tsp	turmeric	½ tsp
1 tsp	salt	1 tsp

Put rice in a large pan of boiling salted water. Cook until just tender, drain well and set aside.

In a large frying pan, heat the oil and gently fry the onions for about 12 minutes until tender and just turning golden.

Turn the heat up and add spices and salt; stir well and cook for 1 further minute.

Tip the rice into the spiced onions and mix together well. Heat through to serve.

PER SERVING	
Calories	320
% Calories from fat	25
Fat (g)	8.9
Saturated fat (g)	0.7
Cholesterol (mg)	0
Sodium (mg)	588
Protein (g)	5.7
Carbohydrate (g)	55.7
Calcium (mg)	65.6
EXCHANGES	
Milk	0.0
Vegetable	0.0
Fruit	0.0
Bread	3.5
Meat	0.0
Fat	1.5

You can make a batch and freeze some for another time.

Yorkshire Puddings

Serves 4

I was surprised at how good these were, and how hard it was to tell that they were not made with cow's milk.

3 tbsps	all-purpose flour	3 tbsps
	pinch of salt	
1	egg	1
½ cup	soy milk	120 ml
	salt and freshly ground pepper	
2 tbsps	vegetable oil	30 ml
	sunflower oil or olive oil for the roasting pan	

You will need a Yorkshire pudding pan (or a cupcake/muffin pan) with about 12 individual holes or 8 larger ones.

Alternatively, make one large pudding in a roasting pan, which will need to be baked longer.

Pre-heat the oven to 425F. Make the batter: sift the flour and salt into a bowl. Make a well in the center of the flour and crack the egg into it. Beat the egg into the flour, then slowly beat in the soy milk until all the flour is incorporated. An electric whisk may be used.

Generously grease the pudding pan with oil in each section. Put the pan in the oven for about 5 minutes until very hot and sizzling. Pour batter into the molds.

Bake for about 15 minutes in the hot oven until well risen, crisp and golden. Serve as soon as possible.

PER SERVING	
Calories	110
% Calories from fat	70
Fat (g)	8.7
Saturated fat (g)	1.3
Cholesterol (mg)	53.1
Sodium (mg)	20
Protein (g)	3
Carbohydrate (g)	5.2
Calcium (mg)	8.2
EXCHANGES	
Milk	0.0
Vegetable	0.0
Fruit	0.0
Bread	0.0
Meat	0.0
Fat	2.0

Savory Sauces and Accompaniments

Aioli Sauce

Basil and Nut Pesto

Chili Bean Salsa

Cider and Wholegrain Mustard Sauce

Creamy Curried Coconut Sauce

Minted Yogurt Sauce

Peanut and Coconut Chili Sauce

Roasted Sweetcorn and Lime Salsa

Roasted Tomato Sauce

Tangy Mayonnaise

Tomato and Mint Salsa

Tomato and Pimiento Coulis

Tomato and Sweet Chili Relish

Velouté Sauce

Bread Sauce

Onion Marmalade

Spiced Walnuts

Cajun Spice Mix

Flour Tortillas (Tortillas de Harina)

If the sauce curdles, remove from the heat and try whisking in a little cold water.

You can now buy concentrated fish stock in liquid form from supermarkets. Vegetable bouillon could be used instead of fish stock.

Aioli Sauce

Serves 8 (2 tablespoons per serving)

This is a lovely creamy garlic sauce, which is very simple and perfect for the lactose-intolerant diner as it uses mayonnaise. It complements many types of fish such as white fish, haddock or salmon.

1³/₄ cups	fish stock	420 ml
2	cloves garlic, crushed	2
1 tsp	arrowroot or other thickener	1 tsp
6 tbsps	low-fat mayonnaise	6 tbsps
1 tbsp	finely chopped parsley	1 tbsp

Bring the stock and the crushed garlic to a boil.

Add the arrowroot and whisk until the mixture begins to thicken.

Remove from heat and allow the pan to cool several minutes before you whisk in the mayonnaise; if the sauce becomes too hot it will curdle.

When the mayonnaise is all whisked in, add the parsley and season.

Warm over very low heat. Spoon over the fish to serve. Makes about 2 cups.

PER SERVING	
Calories	45
% Calories from fat	77
Fat (g)	3.8
Saturated fat (g)	0.7
Cholesterol (mg)	4.2
Sodium (mg)	166
Protein (g)	1.3
Carbohydrate (g)	1.2
Calcium (mg)	4.3
EXCHANGES	
Milk	0.0
Vegetable	0.0
Fruit	0.0
Bread	0.0
Meat	0.0
Fat	1.0

Smoked Trout Chowder
(page 16)

Chive Cream Cheese Dip
(page 20)

Chili Chicken with Basil
and Coconut (page 66)

Celeriac, Walnut and
Apple Salad with Mint
Tofu Mayonnaise
(page 133)

Tangy Citrus Cheesecake
(page 163)

Chocolate Brownies
(page 162)

Blueberry Muffins and Banana Oat Shake
(pages 189 and 192)

Try different variations with different herbs, such as fresh cilantro, and different nuts.

Basil and Nut Pesto

Serves 16 (2 tablespoons per serving)

Most bought pesto contains cheese, usually in the form of Parmesan. I have included here a successful version of my own, which is equally if not more delicious with a fresher taste. It may be stored in the fridge for up to two weeks. Serve with a bowl of pasta for a delicious supper.

1 cup	(scant) extra-virgin olive oil	220 ml
2 tbsps	cashew nuts	2 tbsps
2 tbsps	Brazil nuts	2 tbsps
2	cloves garlic, peeled and roughly chopped	2
1 cup	mixed basil and flat leaf parsley, large stalks removed (3 oz)	85 g
1 tsp	salt	1 tsp
2 tbsps	cider vinegar	30 ml
1 tbsp	lemon juice	15 ml
	freshly ground pepper	

Place all the ingredients in a food processor and blend for 30 seconds; scrape around inside with spatula and process again for a further 30 seconds and taste for seasoning.

Scrape out and store in a screw-top jar.

Use as required. Makes approximately 2 cups.

PER SERVING	
Calories	154
% Calories from fat	91
Fat (g)	15.7
Saturated fat (g)	2.3
Cholesterol (mg)	0
Sodium (mg)	147
Protein (g)	1.2
Carbohydrate (g)	2.4
Calcium (mg)	10.1

EXCHANGES	
Milk	0.0
Vegetable	0.0
Fruit	0.0
Bread	0.0
Meat	0.0
Fat	3.0

This salsa makes a delicious meal with chunks of canned tuna.

Chili Bean Salsa

Serves 6 (¹/₂ cup per serving)

Salsa in Mexico means salad, yet we tend to think of it more as a sauce accompaniment. This version is also a lovely salad in its own right. Varying the types of beans or the peppers gives the salsa a more colorful look. Serve with the Spicy Chicken Quesadillas (see page 49).

1	14-oz can of kidney, butter or pinto beans, drained (2 cups)	1
1	green bell pepper, de-seeded and finely diced	1
1	red chili pepper, seeds removed, finely chopped	1
2	green onions, finely chopped	2
1 tbsp	fresh chopped cilantro	1 tbsp
1 tbsp	lemon juice	15 ml
2 tbsps	olive oil	30 ml
	salt and freshly ground pepper	

Mix all the ingredients together in a bowl and season well. Serve chilled. Makes about 3 cups.

PER SERVING	
Calories	123
% Calories from fat	34
Fat (g)	4.9
Saturated fat (g)	0.7
Cholesterol (mg)	0
Sodium (mg)	293
Protein (g)	4.9
Carbohydrate (g)	15.9
Calcium (mg)	27.4

EXCHANGES	
Milk	0.0
Vegetable	0.0
Fruit	0.0
Bread	1.0
Meat	0.0
Fat	1.0

This sauce would also go very well with chicken, pork and ham dishes.

Cider and Wholegrain Mustard Sauce

Serves 16 (2 tablespoons per serving)

This mouth-watering sauce is adapted from the sauce I make with sugar-baked ham. This version is slightly richer and creamier. Serve hot with the Pork Steak with Hazelnut and Sage Crust on page 78.

2 tsps	vegan margarine	16 g
2 tsps	all-purpose flour	2 tsps
1 cup	(scant) dry cider	220 ml
1/2 cup	chicken or vegetable stock	120 ml
2 tsps	honey	2 tsps
2 tsps	soy sauce	10 ml
1 tbsp	wholegrain mustard	1 tbsp
2/3 cup	soy cream	150 ml
	freshly ground pepper	

Melt the margarine in a large frying pan, add flour and cook several minutes until flour is cooked.

Gradually stir in cider and stock until smooth.

Bring to a boil, stirring well for 3 minutes until sauce thickens. Stir in the honey, soy sauce and mustard.

Finally, pour in soy cream, and season with freshly ground pepper. Gently warm to serve. Makes about 2 cups.

PER SERVING

Calories	26
% Calories from fat	43
Fat (g)	1.2
Saturated fat (g)	0.1
Cholesterol (mg)	0
Sodium (mg)	79
Protein (g)	0.2
Carbohydrate (g)	2.1
Calcium (mg)	3.3

EXCHANGES

Milk	0.0
Vegetable	0.0
Fruit	0.0
Bread	0.0
Meat	0.0
Fat	0.0

For a quick chicken curry, fry strips of chicken breast and add to this sauce.

Creamy Curried Coconut Sauce

Serves 24 (2 tablespoons per serving)

I originally made this to go with kedgeree. However, I now often serve it with salmon or smoked haddock fish cakes for a light supper.

1 tbsp	peanut oil	15 ml
1	medium onion, very finely chopped	1
2 tsps	curry powder	2 tsps
2 tsps	cumin powder	2 tsps
1 tsp	ground turmeric	1 tsp
1 tbsp	all-purpose flour	1 tbsp
1 cup	vegetable stock	240 ml
1	14-oz can reduced-fat coconut milk	1

In a medium-size pan, heat oil and slowly fry onion for about 8 minutes until soft.

Add curry powder, cumin and turmeric and cook for 1 minute, stirring continuously.

Add flour and stir well, slowly incorporating stock until smooth.

Bring to a boil, stirring well, and cook for about 1 minute.

Add coconut milk, heat well and serve. Makes about 3 cups.

Serve warm with Kedgeree on page 191.

PER SERVING	
Calories	22
% Calories from fat	64
Fat (g)	1.6
Saturated fat (g)	0.7
Cholesterol (mg)	0
Sodium (mg)	28
Protein (g)	0.2
Carbohydrate (g)	1.7
Calcium (mg)	4.4
EXCHANGES	
Milk	0.0
Vegetable	0.0
Fruit	0.0
Bread	0.0
Meat	0.0
Fat	0.0

Minted Yogurt Sauce

Serves 8 (2 tablespoons per serving)

This is similar to the sauce found in Indian restaurants served with popadoms. It cools down any hot curry dishes and is ideal as a creamy accompaniment to dry spicy vegetable curries. I have served it with the trout recipe on page 79.

3 tbsps	plain soy yogurt	3 tbsps
3 tbsps	low-fat mayonnaise	3 tbsps
1	heaping teaspoon honey	1
2 tbsps	chopped fresh mint	2 tbsps
	salt and freshly ground pepper	

In a liquidizer or food processor, mix all the above ingredients. Process for about 1 minute until well blended; chill. Serve at room temperature. Makes about 1 cup.

PER SERVING	
Calories	16
% Calories from fat	24
Fat (g)	0.4
Saturated fat (g)	0.1
Cholesterol (mg)	1.1
Sodium (mg)	53
Protein (g)	0.2
Carbohydrate (g)	2.9
Calcium (mg)	21.2
EXCHANGES	
Milk	0.0
Vegetable	0.0
Fruit	0.0
Bread	0.0
Meat	0.0
Fat	0.0

If the sauce becomes too thick, thin it down with a drop of water and mix well. This sauce thickens on cooling, so it needs to be heated through thoroughly before serving.

Peanut and Coconut Chili Sauce

Serves 8 (¹/₄ cup per serving)

This is great for the lactose-intolerant person who feels he or she has been deprived of rich fattening sauces. It is really a satay-style sauce and goes well with chicken or pork kebabs. I have served it with the Marinated Lime and Sesame Chicken Sticks on page 31.

2 tsps	peanut oil	10 ml
1	medium onion, very finely chopped	1
1	clove garlic, peeled and crushed	1
1	red chili pepper, de-seeded and finely chopped	1
²/₃ cup	vegetable or chicken stock	150 ml
2 tbsps	crunchy peanut butter	2 tbsps
²/₃ cup	reduced-fat coconut milk	150 ml
1 tsp	soy sauce	5 ml
1 tbsp	chopped fresh mint or cilantro	1 tbsp
	freshly ground black pepper	

Heat the oil in a small pan, and sauté the onion, garlic and chili for about 5 minutes until soft.

Pour in the stock, and simmer for several minutes.

Next, stir in the peanut butter and mix well.

Pour in coconut milk. Simmer for a few minutes, during which time the sauce should become slightly thicker.

Stir in the soy sauce and mint, mix and season with pepper. Serve warm. Makes about 2 cups.

PER SERVING

Calories	58
% Calories from fat	63
Fat (g)	4.2
Saturated fat (g)	1.3
Cholesterol (mg)	0
Sodium (mg)	10.8
Protein (g)	1.6
Carbohydrate (g)	4
Calcium (mg)	8.3

EXCHANGES

Milk	0.0
Vegetable	0.0
Fruit	0.0
Bread	0.0
Meat	0.0
Fat	1.0

Roasted Sweetcorn and Lime Salsa

Serves 8 (¹/₄ cup per serving)

This is one of my favorite styles of salsa. Broiling the sweetcorn gives a more intense nutty sweetness. This makes a great salad or a delicious accompaniment to Mexican empañadas, enchiladas or tortilla crisps for a snack. It can also be served with barbecued burgers.

2	fresh cobs of corn	2
1	small red onion, finely chopped	1
4	small tomatoes, seeded, finely chopped	4
1	small red chili pepper, seeded, finely chopped	1
2 tbsps	fresh lime juice	30 ml
3 tbsps	olive oil	45 ml
2 tbsps	coarsely chopped fresh cilantro	2 tbsps
	salt and freshly ground pepper	

Pre-heat the broiler. Place the cobs under the heat and toast for about 10 minutes, turning occasionally, until the outside is brown.

When cool, scrape off all the kernels using a sharp knife.

Combine the kernels in a bowl with remaining ingredients, and leave in the fridge for about an hour to allow the flavors to develop.

Season with salt and freshly ground pepper. Serve chilled. Makes about 2 cups.

PER SERVING	
Calories	83
% Calories from fat	55
Fat (g)	5.6
Saturated fat (g)	0.8
Cholesterol (mg)	0
Sodium (mg)	10
Protein (g)	1.5
Carbohydrate (g)	8.6
Calcium (mg)	6.3

EXCHANGES	
Milk	0.0
Vegetable	0.0
Fruit	0.0
Bread	0.5
Meat	0.0
Fat	1.0

Add ham and leeks for a delicious pasta sauce.

Roasted Tomato Sauce

Serves 6 (¹/₂ cup per serving)

This is a rich tomato sauce that goes really well with Italian pasta dishes.

6	medium tomatoes, quartered	6
4	cloves garlic, peeled and left whole	4
1 tbsp	red wine vinegar	15 ml
1 tsp	brown sugar	8 g
1	medium onion, roughly chopped	1
2 tbsps	olive oil	30 ml

Pre-heat the oven to 375F. Mix all the ingredients in a baking dish.

Roast uncovered about 30 minutes until the onions are soft.

Blend or process tomato mixture until smooth; if necessary, thin down with dash of water or tomato juice.

Pass the sauce through a sieve. Warm gently to serve. Makes about 3 cups.

PER SERVING	
Calories	78
% Calories from fat	52
Fat (g)	4.9
Saturated fat (g)	0.7
Cholesterol (mg)	0
Sodium (mg)	12
Protein (g)	1.4
Carbohydrate (g)	8.7
Calcium (mg)	14.1

EXCHANGES	
Milk	0.0
Vegetable	1.0
Fruit	0.0
Bread	0.0
Meat	0.0
Fat	1.0

Liquidize for a smoother sauce.

PER SERVING	
Calories	52
% Calories from fat	68
Fat (g)	4.1
Saturated fat (g)	0.7
Cholesterol (mg)	5.1
Sodium (mg)	165
Protein (g)	0.1
Carbohydrate (g)	4.2
Calcium (mg)	0.8
EXCHANGES	
Milk	0.0
Vegetable	0.0
Fruit	0.0
Bread	0.0
Meat	0.0
Fat	1.0

Tangy Mayonnaise

Serves 12 (2 tablespoons per serving)

This is really similar to tartar sauce and is delicious with most fried fish dishes or fish cakes. Delicious served with the Smoked Fish Cakes on page 89.

2 tbsps	cornichons (small gherkins)	2 tbsps
2 tbsps	drained capers	2 tbsps
1 cup	(scant) low-fat mayonnaise	1 cup
1 tbsp	chopped fresh dill	1 tbsp
1 tbsp	lemon juice	5 ml
	freshly ground pepper	

Finely chop the cornichons and the capers. Combine all the ingredients together in a bowl.

Cover and refrigerate until required. Serve chilled. Makes 1 1/2 cups.

This salsa lasts only up to a day in the fridge. Any longer and the tomatoes tend to lose some of their brightness, and the salsa goes watery.

PER SERVING	
Calories	110
% Calories from fat	56
Fat (g)	7.4
Saturated fat (g)	1
Cholesterol (mg)	0
Sodium (mg)	17
Protein (g)	1.9
Carbohydrate (g)	11.3
Calcium (mg)	18.9
EXCHANGES	
Milk	0.0
Vegetable	2.0
Fruit	0.0
Bread	0.0
Meat	0.0
Fat	1.5

Tomato and Mint Salsa

Serves 6 (1/4 cup per serving)

Most salsas require fresh cilantro, but I have masses of lovely home-grown mint in the summer and often make this to accompany barbecued lamb dishes. Again, like most salsas, it can be a refreshing salad.

8	ripe tomatoes	8
1	large red onion	1
1–2	red chili peppers	1–2
3 tbsps	olive oil	45 ml
	juice from 1 lime	
1 tsp	sugar	8 g
	bunch of fresh mint	
	salt and pepper	

Finely dice tomatoes into medium bowl. Personally, I don't fuss about skinning and de-seeding the tomatoes, as those bits are the best. Makes 1 1/2 cups.

Finely chop the red onion, then de-seed and finely chop the chili. Add to the bowl.

Stir in the olive oil, lime juice, sugar and plenty of freshly chopped mint.

Season with salt and pepper. Refrigerate until required. Serve chilled.

If you prefer, use fresh red bell peppers. Remove the skins by broiling the peppers until charred all over. Then allow them to cool slightly before removing the skins and halving the peppers to remove the seeds.

Tomato and Pimiento Coulis

Serves 14 (¹/₄ cup per serving)

This sauce would be a suitable accompaniment to vegetarian roasts or stuffed vegetables. It is also delicious with meatballs, meat loafs and pasta dishes.

2 tbsps	olive oil	30 ml
2	medium onions, finely chopped	2
2	cloves garlic, crushed	2
1	14-oz can chopped tomatoes	1
1 tbsp	tomato purée	1 tbsp
1	12-oz (approx.) can red pimientos, drained (about 1 cup)	1
1 tsp	sugar	8 g
	salt and freshly ground pepper	
1 tbsp	chopped fresh basil	1 tbsp

Heat the olive oil in a saucepan, and cook onions and garlic for about 5 minutes until soft.

Add tomatoes, tomato purée, drained pimientos and sugar, and cook for a further 5 minutes.

Liquidize, season well and stir in the chopped fresh basil. Serve hot. Makes about 3¹/₂ cups.

PER SERVING	
Calories	38
% Calories from fat	48
Fat (g)	2.1
Saturated fat (g)	0.3
Cholesterol (mg)	0
Sodium (mg)	130
Protein (g)	1
Carbohydrate (g)	4
Calcium (mg)	14.8

EXCHANGES	
Milk	0.0
Vegetable	1.0
Fruit	0.0
Bread	0.0
Meat	0.0
Fat	0.5

Sweet chili sauce containing vinegar, chilies, sugar, garlic and salt is used in Thai cooking. I find it a useful ingredient to keep in the fridge.

PER SERVING	
Calories	35
% Calories from fat	45
Fat (g)	1.9
Saturated fat (g)	0.3
Cholesterol (mg)	0
Sodium (mg)	56
Protein (g)	0.7
Carbohydrate (g)	4.5
Calcium (mg)	5.3
EXCHANGES	
Milk	0.0
Vegetable	1.0
Fruit	0.0
Bread	0.0
Meat	0.0
Fat	0.0

Tomato and Sweet Chili Relish

Serves 8 (¹/₄ cup per serving)

A quick and easy sauce to serve cold with barbecued burgers or sausages. Also great with vegetarian burgers or the Sweet Potato and Chick Pea Cakes on page 59.

4	ripe tomatoes, finely diced	4
1	small red onion, finely chopped	1
1 tbsp	olive oil	15 ml
¹/₂ tbsp	lemon juice	8 ml
2 tbsps	sweet chili sauce	2 tbsps

Mix all the ingredients together and taste; adjust seasoning if necessary.

Serve cold. Makes about 2 cups.

Try this sauce with white fish on a bed of steamed spinach for a healthy, tasty meal.

Add a tablespoon of soy cream to make the sauce slightly richer and creamier.

PER SERVING	
Calories	54
% Calories from fat	73
Fat (g)	4.5
Saturated fat (g)	1
Cholesterol (mg)	0.8
Sodium (mg)	171
Protein (g)	2.1
Carbohydrate (g)	1.5
Calcium (mg)	4.1
EXCHANGES	
Milk	0.0
Vegetable	0.0
Fruit	0.0
Bread	0.0
Meat	0.0
Fat	1.0

Velouté Sauce

Serves 6 (¹/₄ cup per serving)

This is a slightly lower fat sauce, as it uses stock where many sauces use milk and cream. It goes well with broiled or pan-fried fish such as sole, cod, haddock, etc.

2 cups	good quality fish stock	480 ml
2 tbsps	vegan margarine	50 g
1¹/₂ tbsps	all-purpose flour	1¹/₂ tbsps

Bring the fish stock to a boil. Meanwhile, melt the margarine in another pan, add flour and cook gently for about 1 minute.

Allow to cool slightly, then slowly add the hot stock, stirring well until smooth.

Return to the heat and simmer for about 20 minutes, stirring occasionally to avoid sticking.

Serve hot, adding chopped fresh tarragon, dill or chives for a varied flavor. Makes about 1¹/₂ cups.

Bread Sauce

Serves 8 (¹/₄ cup per serving)

This sauce was one that I thought I had better include as it is traditionally served with roast chicken and turkey. Made with soy milk, it is hard to tell it is not the real thing. I challenge anyone to tell the difference.

1 cup	soy milk	240 ml
1	onion, chopped in quarters	1
6	cloves, or ¹/₂ teaspoon powdered cloves	6
2	bay leaves	2
6	black peppercorns	6
	pinch of nutmeg	
	salt	
¹/₄ cup	fresh white breadcrumbs	55 g
1 tbsp	vegan margarine	25 g

Pour soy milk into a saucepan, and add the onion, cloves, bay leaves, peppercorns, nutmeg and salt.

Heat over low heat for about 10 minutes to infuse the flavors into the soy milk.

Bring mixture to a higher temperature, but not boiling; remove from heat and leave to stand for a further 5 minutes.

Strain the sauce onto the breadcrumbs and, mixing well, add the margarine; check for seasoning.

If it appears too thick, add a little more soy milk. Serve warm or cool. Makes about 2 cups.

PER SERVING

Calories	36
% Calories from fat	51
Fat (g)	2.1
Saturated fat (g)	0.4
Cholesterol (mg)	0
Sodium (mg)	29
Protein (g)	1.3
Carbohydrate (g)	3.3
Calcium (mg)	11.5

EXCHANGES

Milk	0.0
Vegetable	0.0
Fruit	0.0
Bread	0.5
Meat	0.0
Fat	0.0

A nice filling for baked potatoes or with smoked ham.
  Make with red onions for a bit more depth in color.

Onion Marmalade

Serves 18 (2 tablespoons per serving)

I sometimes make a batch of this marmalade, as it stores well in a jar in the fridge for several weeks. It is delicious served with the Smoked Duck Salad on page 32. It is also particularly good with cold meats or pâtés in light lunch. For anyone who can eat goat's and sheep's cheese, the marmalade makes a delicious combination with either cold or grilled cheese.

5	large onions, each weighing about 8 oz, halved and sliced in half rings	5
1 tbsp	sunflower oil	15 ml
2/3 cup	red wine	150 ml
2/3 cup	balsamic vinegar	150 ml
2 tbsps	light brown sugar	50 g
1/4 cup	water	60 ml
1/2 tsp	salt	1/2 tsp

In a large frying pan or saucepan, heat the oil and add the onions.
  Sauté over gentle heat for about 10 minutes, stirring continuously until the onions are almost soft; make sure they do not burn.
  Reduce the heat, and add red wine, vinegar, sugar, water and salt.
  Stir well, cover pan and simmer for about 30 minutes, adding a few spoons of water if it dries out.
  Remove lid and, stirring occasionally, cook for a further 5 minutes.
  The marmalade should still be moist with a tiny bit of thick liquid.
  Fill a large jar with boiling water, let rest for a few minutes and empty.
  Fill jar with onion marmalade and close lid firmly.
  Allow to cool and then refrigerate. Makes about 2 1/4 cups.

PER SERVING	
Calories	36
% Calories from fat	20
Fat (g)	0.8
Saturated fat (g)	0.1
Cholesterol (mg)	0
Sodium (mg)	66
Protein (g)	0.4
Carbohydrate (g)	5.5
Calcium (mg)	8.1

EXCHANGES	
Milk	0.0
Vegetable	1.0
Fruit	0.0
Bread	0.0
Meat	0.0
Fat	0.0

Garam masala is an Indian spice that may be found in ethnic aisles or at Indian grocery stores.

Spiced Walnuts

Serves 16 (2 tablespoons per serving)

This recipe works equally well made with whole almonds or cashew nuts and served as a great little snack. Also try mixing lots of varieties of spiced nuts in a large bowl when friends come around for drinks. Serve with Smoked Duck Salad on page 32.

1 tbsp	olive oil	15 ml
1 tsp	Chinese 5 spice powder	1 tsp
1 tsp	garam masala	1 tsp
2 cups	walnut halves	2 cups
1½ tsp	superfine sugar	12 g
½ tsp	salt	½ tsp

Heat the oil in a large frying pan over medium heat.
Add the spices, stirring well, and cook for 30 seconds.
Stir in the walnuts, followed by the sugar and salt.
Shake the pan continuously and cook for 1 further minute over low heat. Allow to cool. Makes about 2 cups.

PER SERVING	
Calories	108
% Calories from fat	83
Fat (g)	10.6
Saturated fat (g)	1
Cholesterol (mg)	0
Sodium (mg)	73
Protein (g)	2.3
Carbohydrate (g)	2.6
Calcium (mg)	16.5

EXCHANGES	
Milk	0.0
Vegetable	0.0
Fruit	0.0
Bread	0.0
Meat	0.0
Fat	2.5

Delicious with chicken and fish dishes.

Cajun Spice Mix

Serves 12 (1 tsp per serving)

Since I have included a few Cajun dishes in this book, I thought I would include a recipe for Cajun Spice Mix. It can be bought from most supermarkets, but this homemade version tastes better and has no salt.

1 tbsp	garlic powder (if unavailable use 4 cloves fresh garlic, crushed)	1 tbsp
1 tbsp	onion powder	1 tbsp
2 tsps	cracked black pepper	2 tsps
1 tsp	dried cumin	1 tsp
1 1/2 tsps	cayenne pepper	1 1/2 tsps
1/2 tsp	allspice	1/2 tsp
1 tsp	dried oregano	1 tsp
1 tsp	dried thyme	1 tsp

Mix the spices together and store in a jar. If you use fresh garlic, you will need about 4 cloves crushed to a paste, and the spice mix will then become a paste rather than a powder, in which case store it in the fridge.

Use as required in Cajun recipes. Makes about 1/4 cup.

PER SERVING	
Calories	8
% Calories from fat	13
Fat (g)	0.1
Saturated fat (g)	0
Cholesterol (mg)	0
Sodium (mg)	1
Protein (g)	0.3
Carbohydrate (g)	1.6
Calcium (mg)	10.7
EXCHANGES	
Milk	0.0
Vegetable	0.0
Fruit	0.0
Bread	0.0
Meat	0.0
Fat	0.0

A friend of mine recently used tortillas as wraps. This was a great idea, as once smothered in a sauce, they resemble crepes with slightly more texture.

Flour Tortillas (Tortillas de Harina)

Makes 12 tortillas

I find that the tortillas in the supermarket contain many unnecessary ingredients. The homemade variety is not only healthier but also a lot cheaper and fun to make. The other types of tortillas are made with masa harina, which is corn flour specially treated for tortillas. To make them, use 5 oz masa harina, pinch salt and 4 fl oz warm water; make pliable dough, rest for 20 minutes then proceed as with flour tortillas.

1¼ cups	all-purpose white flour	1¼ cups
2 tsps	salt	2 tsps
½ cup	white lard, cut into small pieces	110 g
7 tbsps	warm water	105 ml

Sieve the flour and salt into a large bowl. Rub in the fat until the mixture resembles breadcrumbs.

Gradually add the warm water until you have pliable dough. Knead for 5 minutes.

Divide into 12 balls and cover them with a damp cloth.

On a floured surface, roll each ball into a circle approximately 9 inches in diameter. The dough should be very thin.

Heat a large, heavy frying pan over medium heat and cook each tortilla, turning once.

Count to about 40 as you cook each side. Tortillas should come out lightly spotted with brown.

Stack the cooked tortillas with waxed paper between each one. Warm as recipe instructs before using.

PER SERVING	
Calories	123
% Calories from fat	63
Fat (g)	8.5
Saturated fat (g)	3.3
Cholesterol (mg)	8
Sodium (mg)	388
Protein (g)	1.3
Carbohydrate (g)	9.9
Calcium (mg)	2.2

EXCHANGES	
Milk	0.0
Vegetable	0.0
Fruit	0.0
Bread	1.0
Meat	0.0
Fat	1.5

Salads and Dressings

Chicken, Avocado and Watercress Salad

Bulgur Wheat Salad

Carrot and Sesame Salad

Celeriac, Walnut and Apple Salad with Mint Tofu Mayonnaise

Crisp Chinese Salad

Cucumber, Mint and Soy Yogurt Salad

Red Cabbage and Pumpkin Seed Coleslaw

Roasted Fennel and Beet Salad

Roasted Vegetable and Tuna Rice Salad

Warm Sweet Potato and Artichoke Salad

Tarragon French Dressing

Creamy Lemon Dressing

Creamy Tahini Dressing

Harissa Dressing

Lime and Cilantro Dressing

Oriental Sesame Dressing

Sun-Dried Tomato, Basil and Garlic Dressing

Tofu Mayonnaise

Even better, if you can use smoked chicken, this would be delicious. For a vegetarian alternative, omit chicken and add a handful of walnuts.

Chicken, Avocado and Watercress Salad

Serves 4

This makes a quick and tasty lunch if you have any spare chicken in your fridge, but prepare it just before serving, as the avocado will start to discolor. Delicious served with brown rice or crunchy bread. Also try it as a filling for hot pita bread or on a baguette for a lunchtime sandwich. Baby spinach would be equally as tasty as watercress.

1 cup	diced skinless cooked chicken	220 g
2	green onions, thinly sliced	2
1/2	large ripe avocado	1/2
1/2 recipe	Creamy Tahini Dressing (see page 141)	1/2 recipe
	salt and freshly ground pepper	
3–4 cups	watercress	3–4 cups

Mix chicken, green onions and avocado, then stir in the dressing. Season with salt and pepper and serve on a bed of watercress.

PER SERVING	
Calories	236
% Calories from fat	75
Fat (g)	20.1
Saturated fat (g)	2.5
Cholesterol (mg)	27.9
Sodium (mg)	57
Protein (g)	11.6
Carbohydrate (g)	3.5
Calcium (mg)	45.6
EXCHANGES	
Milk	0.0
Vegetable	0.0
Fruit	0.0
Bread	0.0
Meat	1.0
Fat	4.0

Check the preparation instructions on the packet of bulgur wheat, as brands may vary.

Bulgur Wheat Salad

Serves 6–8

This refreshing summer salad is a variation of the traditional Middle Eastern salad, tabbouleh. It may seem that there is a lot of mint and parsley in the recipe; this adds to the character of the salad.

1 cup	bulgur wheat	220 g
1 tsp	salt	1 tsp
2 cups	boiling water	480 ml
1/4 cup	olive oil	60 ml
3 tbsps	lemon juice	45 ml
1/2	cucumber	1/2
3	firm tomatoes	3
1	red bell pepper, de-seeded	1
4	green onions	4
3 tbsps	chopped fresh mint	3 tbsps
1/4 cup	chopped fresh parsley	4 tbsps
	salt and pepper	

Mix the bulgur wheat with the salt and boiling water. Leave it for about 20 minutes until the wheat is tender. Drain off any excess water and allow to dry out.

Mix the bulgur wheat with the lemon and olive oil, and refrigerate for several hours if possible at this point to allow the wheat to soak up the flavors.

Just before serving, chop the cucumber, tomatoes and bell pepper into small dice.

Finely chop the green onions and include the green parts.

Mix the chopped vegetables and herbs with the bulgur wheat. Season with salt and pepper. Serve chilled.

PER SERVING	
Calories	188
% Calories from fat	43
Fat (g)	9.6
Saturated fat (g)	1.3
Cholesterol (mg)	0
Sodium (mg)	401
Protein (g)	4.1
Carbohydrate (g)	24.4
Calcium (mg)	30

EXCHANGES	
Milk	0.0
Vegetable	1.0
Fruit	0.0
Bread	1.0
Meat	0.0
Fat	2.0

Substitute 1 tablespoon of the oil for sesame oil to give a fuller-flavored dressing.

Any leftover salad could be used in a sandwich with hummus or in pita bread.

Carrot and Sesame Salad

Serves 4–6

A quick and easy salad to prepare. The carrots and sesame seeds mixed with a tahini dressing are a delightful combination. Serve as part of a buffet.

6–8	medium carrots (about 1 lb)	450 g
2	ribs celery, chopped	2
3	green onions, finely sliced	3
2 tbsps	lemon juice	30 ml
3 tbsps	peanut oil	45 ml
1 tsp	tahini	1 tsp
½ tsp	honey (optional)	½ tsp
2 tbsps	toasted sesame seeds	2 tbsps
	salt and freshly ground pepper	

Peel carrots and grate into a bowl. Mix with the celery and green onions.

In a separate bowl, combine the dressing ingredients with 1 tablespoon of the sesame seeds.

Season with salt and pepper. Add dressing to the mixed carrot, celery and green onion.

Mix well and serve chilled sprinkled with remaining sesame seeds.

PER SERVING	
Calories	178
% Calories from fat	63
Fat (g)	13.2
Saturated fat (g)	2.2
Cholesterol (mg)	0
Sodium (mg)	61
Protein (g)	2.8
Carbohydrate (g)	14.4
Calcium (mg)	54.3
EXCHANGES	
Milk	0.0
Vegetable	3.0
Fruit	0.0
Bread	0.0
Meat	0.0
Fat	2.5

This could also be made with egg-based mayonnaise.

Celeriac, Walnut and Apple Salad with Mint Tofu Mayonnaise

Serves 6

Celeriac gives the salad an interesting crunchiness. The salad should be made just before serving to prevent the apple and celeriac from discoloring. Serve with hot bread or new potatoes for a delicious, nutritious lunch.

¹/₂	celeriac, peeled and cut into small chunks	¹/₂
2–3	apples, cored and cut into small chunks	2–3
¹/₂ cup	roughly chopped walnuts	¹/₂ cup
1 tbsp	chopped fresh mint	1 tbsp
1 tbsp	chopped fresh parsley	1 tbsp
	salt and freshly ground pepper	
¹/₂ recipe	Tofu Mayonnaise (see page 144)	¹/₂ recipe

Mix all salad ingredients with tofu mayonnaise. Serve chilled.

PER SERVING	
Calories	167
% Calories from fat	70
Fat (g)	13.8
Saturated fat (g)	1.4
Cholesterol (mg)	0
Sodium (mg)	141
Protein (g)	3.2
Carbohydrate (g)	9.9
Calcium (mg)	28.9

EXCHANGES	
Milk	0.0
Vegetable	0.0
Fruit	0.5
Bread	0.0
Meat	0.0
Fat	3.0

Try using Chinese cabbage, regular cabbage, cauliflower or broccoli.

PER SERVING	
Calories	172
% Calories from fat	64
Fat (g)	12.6
Saturated fat (g)	2
Cholesterol (mg)	0
Sodium (mg)	546
Protein (g)	3
Carbohydrate (g)	13.2
Calcium (mg)	82
EXCHANGES	
Milk	0.0
Vegetable	2.0
Fruit	0.0
Bread	0.0
Meat	0.0
Fat	3.0

Crisp Chinese Salad

Serves 4

This is a very colorful salad that can be made with a variety of raw vegetables.

2	large carrots, peeled	2
1/2	cucumber	1/2
6	green onions	6
1	red bell pepper	1
2–3 cups	bean sprouts (about 8 oz)	225 g
1 recipe	Oriental Sesame Dressing (see page 143)	1 recipe

Cut the carrot and cucumber into thin julienne strips, similar in length to the bean sprouts.

Discard the outer leaves of the green onion, keeping as much of the green as possible, and shred into similar strips.

Cut the bell pepper in half and remove seeds; cut into thin strips.

Mix everything with the bean sprouts.

Chill and toss with the dressing just before serving.

Cucumber, Mint and Soy Yogurt Salad

Serves 2

This refreshing salad is based on Greek tzatziki. It is ideal as a salad or as an accompaniment to dishes such as Sweet Potato and Chick Pea Cakes (page 59) or served with spicy dishes and barbecues.

1 1/2 cups	soy yogurt	1 1/2 cups
1/2	cucumber, chopped into small cubes	1/2
2 tbsps	chopped fresh mint	2 tbsps
1/2 tsp	honey	1/2 tsp
	salt and freshly ground pepper	

PER SERVING	
Calories	129
% Calories from fat	19
Fat (g)	2.7
Saturated fat (g)	0
Cholesterol (mg)	0
Sodium (mg)	32
Protein (g)	4.3
Carbohydrate (g)	21.8
Calcium (mg)	539.5
EXCHANGES	
Milk	0.5
Vegetable	2.0
Fruit	0.0
Bread	0.0
Meat	0.0
Fat	0.5

Mix all the ingredients and season well.

Refrigerate before serving. Serves 2 as a salad or enough for 4 as an accompaniment.

Red Cabbage and Pumpkin Seed Coleslaw

Serves 4–6

A lovely crisp salad full of goodness.

1/4 head	red cabbage (about 8 oz)	225 g
1	fennel bulb (about 4 oz)	112 g
2–3	carrots, peeled (about 6 oz)	170 g
1	red apple	1
2 tbsps	pumpkin seeds (could use sunflower seeds)	2 tbsps
1/2 recipe	Tarragon French Dressing (page 139)	1/2 recipe
2 tbsps	soy yogurt	2 tbsps

Wash and prepare the cabbage; remove the tough outer leaves and central core if it is too tough, and shred finely.

Shred the fennel, discarding the tough outer leaves.

Grate the carrots and mix in a large bowl with the cabbage and fennel.

Wash and core the apple, and cut into small dice, leaving the skin on for color.

Add the pumpkin seeds to the bowl. Toss everything together with the dressing and the yogurt.

Chill and serve.

PER SERVING	
Calories	325
% Calories from fat	76
Fat (g)	28.1
Saturated fat (g)	2.9
Cholesterol (mg)	0
Sodium (mg)	283
Protein (g)	2.3
Carbohydrate (g)	18.1
Calcium (mg)	85.8

EXCHANGES	
Milk	0.0
Vegetable	1.0
Fruit	0.0
Bread	1.0
Meat	0.0
Fat	5.0

Roasted Fennel and Beet Salad

Serves 4

Roasting fennel and beets is one of the best ways to cook these vegetables. If you are not keen on either vegetable, you may be pleasantly surprised. The roasting juices from the tomatoes combined with the beet, olive oil and vinegar make a delicious red dressing. Serve warm with steamed couscous and nut burgers or tofu fritters. Alternatively, serve with hot bread.

2	large beets	2
1	large or 2 small fennel bulbs	1
2 tbsps	olive oil	30 ml
2	medium tomatoes, cut into 8 wedges	2
4	green onions, cut into 1/2-inch slices	4
1 tbsp	balsamic vinegar	15 ml
	salt and freshly ground pepper	
3	sprigs fresh thyme	3
1 tbsp	fresh parsley	1 tbsp

Pre-heat the oven to 400F. Peel the beets and cut into segments about 1/2 inch across.

Trim the fennel and cut into segments similar size to beets. Place the beets and fennel in a large baking dish, pour over olive oil and shake well in the oil to get a good coating.

Roast in the hot oven for about 25 minutes until the vegetables are beginning to brown at the edges.

Add tomato wedges, onions and balsamic, and mix well. Return to oven for about 15 minutes.

Season with salt and pepper and sprinkle over with thyme leaves and chopped parsley.

If required, drizzle extra olive oil over the salad. Serve warm or chilled.

PER SERVING	
Calories	118
% Calories from fat	51
Fat (g)	7.2
Saturated fat (g)	1
Cholesterol (mg)	0
Sodium (mg)	71
Protein (g)	2.3
Carbohydrate (g)	13.1
Calcium (mg)	57.7
EXCHANGES	
Milk	0.0
Vegetable	2.0
Fruit	0.0
Bread	0.0
Meat	0.0
Fat	1.5

Substitute pasta instead of rice for a delicious pasta salad.

Roasted Vegetable and Tuna Rice Salad

Serves 4

This is perfect for a tasty summer lunch eaten outdoors. The vegetables should all slightly caramelize, giving an added natural sweetness. Serve with some salad leaves or watercress and the Sun-Dried Tomato, Basil and Garlic Dressing.

1	large red bell pepper	1
1	medium red onion	1
1 tbsp	olive oil and extra to drizzle	15 ml
1	clove garlic, crushed	1
	salt and pepper	
1/2 cup	baby corn (about 4 oz)	110 g
4 cups	cooked brown short-grain rice	4 cups
1	can tuna, water packed, drained weight 5 1/4 oz	1
2 recipes	Sun-Dried Tomato, Basil and Garlic Dressing (see page 143)	2 recipes

Heat the broiler, and when it is hot, place the whole red pepper underneath and leave for about 4 minutes before turning. Repeat until completely blistered and black (about 4 turns). Place the pepper in a small plastic bag.

Peel when cool enough to handle, removing seeds and stalk, and cut into chunks; leave to one side.

Peel the red onion, cube and pull layers apart; mix with the olive oil, garlic, salt and pepper in an oven dish.

Leave a gap on one side and lay the baby corn out next to the onions; drizzle over a little more olive oil.

Broil for about 5 minutes, turning from time to time. Add the peppers and mix with the onions. Continue broiling for a further 5 minutes until the baby corn is golden brown and the onions are soft and beginning to caramelize at the edges.

Allow to cool.

In a large bowl, mix the rice with the peppers, onions, baby corn and tuna chunks, and season well with salt and freshly ground pepper.

Refrigerate until needed. To serve, toss with the dressing.

PER SERVING	
Calories	455
% Calories from fat	37
Fat (g)	19
Saturated fat (g)	2.7
Cholesterol (mg)	11.2
Sodium (mg)	308
Protein (g)	16
Carbohydrate (g)	55.2
Calcium (mg)	45

EXCHANGES	
Milk	0.0
Vegetable	2.0
Fruit	0.0
Bread	3.0
Meat	2.0
Fat	2.0

Marinated artichoke hearts are found in most supermarkets and have a wonderful rich flavor.

Warm Sweet Potato and Artichoke Salad

Serves 4

This is an unusual salad, which served with warm crusty bread makes a delicious light lunch. Alternatively, it could be served alongside grilled meat or fish.

3–4	sweet potatoes, peeled but left whole (about 1 lb)	450 g
1 tbsp	olive oil	15 ml
	salt and freshly ground pepper	
1 cup	artichoke hearts packed in oil, drained	1 cup
2–3 cups	watercress, washed and thick stalks removed	2–3 cups
2–3 cups	crisp romaine lettuce, broken up	2–3 cups
2 tbsps	pine nuts	2 tbsps
1½ tbsps	balsamic vinegar	23 ml

Boil or steam the sweet potatoes for about 10 minutes, until firm but almost tender.

Slice into 3/4-inch-thick discs. Coat in the olive oil and season well.

Heat a skillet and fry the potato slices in batches for about 2 minutes either side, until charred.

Slice the artichoke hearts in quarters and quickly warm in the skillet.

Combine the watercress and romaine in a large salad bowl.

Toss the warm potatoes, artichoke hearts and pine nuts together and tip over the leaves.

Mix 4 tablespoons of the artichoke oil from the jar with the balsamic vinegar, season with salt and freshly ground pepper, whisk well and drizzle over salad before serving.

PER SERVING	
Calories	206
% Calories from fat	40
Fat (g)	9.9
Saturated fat (g)	0.9
Cholesterol (mg)	0
Sodium (mg)	182
Protein (g)	3.5
Carbohydrate (g)	29.9
Calcium (mg)	52

EXCHANGES	
Milk	0.0
Vegetable	2.0
Fruit	0.0
Bread	1.0
Meat	0.0
Fat	2.0

Add any other fresh herbs or garlic for a different flavor.

Tarragon French Dressing

Serves 12 (2 tablespoons per serving)

This produces a slightly white and creamy dressing, which should stay thick and not need shaking before serving. The dressing lasts for up to a week in the fridge. Serve with crisp mixed leaf salads.

2 tbsps	Dijon mustard	2 tbsps
2 tbsps	apple cider vinegar	30 ml
1/2 tsp	salt	1/2 tsp
1 cup	(scant) sunflower oil	220 ml
1–2 tbsps	water	15–30 ml
2 tbsps	chopped fresh tarragon	2 tbsps
	freshly ground pepper	

In a medium bowl, whisk the mustard, vinegar and salt together.

Gradually add the oil, beating well to form an emulsion as if making mayonnaise.

When all the oil has been added, the dressing will appear quite thick.

Stir in the water to thin the dressing down, followed by the tarragon and freshly ground pepper.

Store in a sealed jar in the fridge until required. Makes about 1 1/2 cups.

PER SERVING	
Calories	164
% Calories from fat	99
Fat (g)	18.1
Saturated fat (g)	1.9
Cholesterol (mg)	0
Sodium (mg)	154
Protein (g)	0
Carbohydrate (g)	0.2
Calcium (mg)	1.6

EXCHANGES	
Milk	0.0
Vegetable	0.0
Fruit	0.0
Bread	0.0
Meat	0.0
Fat	3.5

I have also made this with limes, which is great with fish dishes such as Thai fish cakes. Try using honey instead of sugar.

Creamy Lemon Dressing

Serves 12 (2 tbsps per serving)

This will have a milky white appearance and a delicious, slightly tangy flavor that adds a special touch to many fish dishes such as fish mousses, crab cakes or fresh crab and lobster.

2	large lemons	2
1 tbsp	sugar	25 g
1/2 tsp	salt	1/2 tsp
1 cup	oil such as sunflower or vegetable	240 ml
	freshly ground pepper	

Using a sharp knife, cut tops and bottoms off the lemons, then moving from top to bottom, cut the lemon skins off and cut out the individual segments, ensuring there are no seeds or pith remaining.

Process the lemon segments, sugar and salt in a blender until smooth and slightly white.

Slowly add the oil while machine is running.

Taste and season with pepper and add more oil if necessary (depends on size of lemons). Makes about 1 1/2 cups.

PER SERVING	
Calories	168
% Calories from fat	93
Fat (g)	18.2
Saturated fat (g)	1.9
Cholesterol (mg)	0
Sodium (mg)	97
Protein (g)	0.2
Carbohydrate (g)	2.9
Calcium (mg)	2.8
EXCHANGES	
Milk	0.0
Vegetable	0.0
Fruit	0.0
Bread	0.0
Meat	0.0
Fat	3.5

Creamy Tahini Dressing

Serves 8 (2 tablespoons per serving)

This dressing is quite similar to Tarragon French Dressing, but the addition of mayonnaise and tahini makes it suitable for rice, beans and pasta salads.

2 tbsps	low-fat mayonnaise	2 tbsps
1 tbsp	apple cider vinegar	15 ml
1 tbsp	tahini	1 tbsp
1/2 cup	sunflower oil	120 ml
1/4 cup	cold water (or more for a thinner dressing)	60 ml
	salt and freshly ground pepper	

Whisk mayonnaise in a bowl with vinegar and tahini.

Gradually add the sunflower oil, whisking well until thick and smooth.

Thin down with the water and season with salt and pepper. Chill to serve. Makes about 1 cup.

PER SERVING	
Calories	141
% Calories from fat	96
Fat (g)	15.4
Saturated fat (g)	1.7
Cholesterol (mg)	1
Sodium (mg)	21
Protein (g)	0.3
Carbohydrate (g)	1.2
Calcium (mg)	2.8

EXCHANGES	
Milk	0.0
Vegetable	0.0
Fruit	0.0
Bread	0.0
Meat	0.0
Fat	3.0

Harissa Dressing

Serves 4 (2 tablespoons per serving)

Harissa is a fiery North African paste made from a mixture of chilies, tomato and garlic with various spices. Here I have made it into a dressing using sun-dried tomato paste, which I think adds a richer flavor. The dressing is delicious with roasted vegetables and couscous. Also great served with the Moroccan Lamb Burgers on page 41 and Spiced Rice on page 109.

1 tbsp	tomato purée	1 tbsp
1 tbsp	sun-dried tomato paste	1 tbsp
1	clove garlic, crushed	1
1 tbsp	ground cumin powder	1 tbsp
1 tsp	ground cilantro powder	1 tsp
1/2 tsp	chili powder	1/2 tsp
2	limes, squeezed	2
1/4 cup	olive oil	60 ml

Mix all the above ingredients well before serving. Makes 1/2 cup.

PER SERVING	
Calories	139
% Calories from fat	88
Fat (g)	13.9
Saturated fat (g)	1.8
Cholesterol (mg)	0
Sodium (mg)	47
Protein (g)	0.8
Carbohydrate (g)	3.6
Calcium (mg)	23.3

EXCHANGES	
Milk	0.0
Vegetable	0.0
Fruit	0.0
Bread	0.0
Meat	0.0
Fat	3.0

Fish sauce is a Thai alternative to soy sauce or salt, made from anchovy extract; if you are unable to find it, substitute a light soy sauce.

Lime and Cilantro Dressing

Serves 4 (2 tablespoons per serving)

This is a delicate Thai-style dressing that goes very well with fish dishes. Serve with monkfish and shrimp kebabs or just plain broiled fish and salad. Prepare dressing up to three days in advance.

3	limes	3
	peanut oil	
	handful of fresh cilantro	
1 tbsp	fish sauce (nam pla)	15 ml
1 inch	fresh gingerroot, peeled and finely chopped	2.5 cm
1	red chili pepper, de-seeded and finely chopped	1
2 tsps	sugar	16 g

Using a vegetable peeler, remove about 6 strips of lime zest, cut these into thin strips, then chop finely.

Squeeze the juice from the limes and pour it into a bowl with an equal amount of peanut oil.

Remove leaves from the cilantro, cut the stalks finely and chop the leaves.

Mix all the ingredients, including the zest. Stir thoroughly, taste and adjust seasoning if necessary. Dressing should be quite tangy, with enough sugar to cut acidity.

Refrigerate until needed. Makes about 1/2 cup.

PER SERVING	
Calories	201
% Calories from fat	88
Fat (g)	20.3
Saturated fat (g)	3.4
Cholesterol (mg)	0
Sodium (mg)	349
Protein (g)	0.6
Carbohydrate (g)	5.6
Calcium (mg)	6.3
EXCHANGES	
Milk	0.0
Vegetable	1.0
Fruit	0.0
Bread	0.0
Meat	0.0
Fat	4.0

If you don't have rice vinegar, cider or white wine vinegar will be fine.

PER SERVING	
Calories	134
% Calories from fat	82
Fat (g)	12.4
Saturated fat (g)	1.9
Cholesterol (mg)	0
Sodium (mg)	515
Protein (g)	1.3
Carbohydrate (g)	4.9
Calcium (mg)	45.7
EXCHANGES	
Milk	0.0
Vegetable	0.0
Fruit	0.0
Bread	0.0
Meat	0.0
Fat	3.0

The dressing may appear to separate slightly from the oil; just mix well before serving.

For a super vegan starter, serve with crisp French bread croutons topped with griddled slithers of mixed vegetables, such as asparagus, peppers, courgettes and aubergine.

PER SERVING	
Calories	51
% Calories from fat	92
Fat (g)	5.4
Saturated fat (g)	0.7
Cholesterol (mg)	0
Sodium (mg)	26
Protein (g)	0.2
Carbohydrate (g)	0.9
Calcium (mg)	3.1
EXCHANGES	
Milk	0.0
Vegetable	0.0
Fruit	0.0
Bread	0.0
Meat	0.0
Fat	1.0

Oriental Sesame Dressing

Serves 4 (2 tablespoons per serving)

This is a delicious dressing that will jazz up any crisp vegetable salad. The addition of sesame seeds and honey adds a lovely nutty sweetness.

2 tsps	honey	2 tsps
2 tbsps	rice vinegar	30 ml
3 tsps	sesame oil	15 ml
2 tbsps	peanut oil	30 ml
2 tbsps	soy sauce	30 ml
2 tbsps	toasted sesame seeds	2 tbsps

Thin the honey down with the rice vinegar until smooth.
Add the oils and soy sauce and taste.
Before serving, mix in toasted sesame seeds. Makes about 1/2 cup.

Sun-Dried Tomato, Basil and Garlic Dressing

Serves 5 (1 tablespoon per serving)

Great served with roasted vegetables. It has a delightful Italian flavor. Serve with the Grilled Fresh Tuna on Potato Niçoise on page 50.

1 tbsp	sun-dried tomato paste	1 tbsp
1	clove garlic, crushed	1
1 tbsp	red wine vinegar	15 ml
2 tbsps	olive oil	30 ml
1 tbsp	fresh basil	1 tbsp
	salt and freshly ground pepper	

Mix sun-dried tomato paste, garlic and vinegar together.
Slowly beat in the oil, then taste and season with basil and salt and pepper. Add more oil if necessary, depending on taste. Makes about 1/3 cup.

This dressing will store in a sealed jar for several days in the fridge.

Tofu Mayonnaise

Serves 8 (2 tablespoons per serving)

Although egg mayonnaise is acceptable for the lactose-free diet, this tofu mayonnaise is more nutritious and slightly lower in fat—especially good for a vegetarian diet.

1	pack (8 3/4 oz) silken tofu	1
2 tsps	wholegrain or Dijon mustard	2 tsps
1	clove fresh garlic (optional)	1
1/2 tsp	salt	1/2 tsp
	freshly ground pepper	
1 tbsp	white wine vinegar or lemon juice	15 ml
6 tbsps	sunflower oil	90 ml

Blend tofu, mustard, garlic, salt, pepper and 1 teaspoon vinegar in a processor.

Gradually pour in the oil and continue blending until smooth and creamy.

Add remaining vinegar and mix thoroughly. Taste for seasoning and serve. Makes about 1 cup.

PER SERVING	
Calories	104
% Calories from fat	91
Fat (g)	10.5
Saturated fat (g)	1.1
Cholesterol (mg)	0
Sodium (mg)	191
Protein (g)	2
Carbohydrate (g)	0.4
Calcium (mg)	13.1

EXCHANGES	
Milk	0.0
Vegetable	0.0
Fruit	0.0
Bread	0.0
Meat	0.0
Fat	2.0

Desserts and Sweet Sauces

Apricot and Almond Fool

Apricot Tart Tatin

Baked Apple Charlotte

Baked Chocolate and Almond Torte

Baked Orange Semolina Puddings

Banana Fritters

Caramelized Apple Pie

Chocolate, Prune and Whiskey Bread Pudding

Coconut Crème Caramel

Coffee Zabaglione

Fresh Raspberry Tart

Honey-Glazed Pineapple and
Fig Kebabs with Orange Sabayon

Mixed Berry and Peach Coconut Crumble

Pear and Ginger Upside Down Cake

Raisin, Lemon and Almond Rice Pudding

Rhubarb and Almond Tart

Chocolate Brownies

Tangy Citrus Cheesecake

Chocolate Fudge Sauce

Pastry Cream

Custard Sauce

Fresh Raspberry Coulis

Rich Butterscotch Sauce

Mocha Chocolate Sauce

Oat and Honey Cream

Tofu and Almond Cream

You could make this using either different dried fruit or fresh fruit.

Apricot and Almond Fool

Serves 4

This is a quick and simple vegan pudding. It contains lots of goodness in the almonds and the apricots. Try it on the children to jazz up soy yogurt. Serve with crisp cookies or macaroons.

2 cups	dried apricots, two reserved and chopped (about 1/2 lb)	225 g
1 cup	boiling water	240 ml
1 cup	soy yogurt	1 cup
2/3 cup	blanched almonds (3 oz)	85 g
1 tbsp	maple syrup	15 ml
1/2 tsp	vanilla extract	1/2 tsp

Cover the apricots with the boiling water and soak overnight, or, alternatively, simmer in the water until soft.

Purée the apricots in the soaking liquid until smooth and allow to cool. When cold, fold in the yogurt.

Grind the almonds finely in a food processor or grinder, add enough water to make a thick cream and continue grinding until smooth.

Sweeten with maple syrup and vanilla extract.

Add the apricot purée and blend until smooth.

Spoon into four small dishes. Decorate with chopped apricots. Refrigerate before serving.

PER SERVING	
Calories	385
% Calories from fat	29
Fat (g)	13.5
Saturated fat (g)	1
Cholesterol (mg)	0
Sodium (mg)	25
Protein (g)	9.5
Carbohydrate (g)	64
Calcium (mg)	267.2

EXCHANGES	
Milk	0.0
Vegetable	0.0
Fruit	4.0
Bread	0.0
Meat	0.0
Fat	3.0

I have made this pudding with a variety of different fruits: apples, quinces, bananas, fresh or canned pineapple and pears with crystallized ginger, which was scrumptious.

Apricot Tart Tatin

Serves 8

This is one of my favorites, as it can be prepared in advance and cooked before serving. The pastry is deliciously crisp. Serve it with soy ice cream or soy yogurt. For an even healthier option, serve it with the Oat and Honey Cream or the Tofu and Almond Cream (see pages 169, 170).

Pastry

³/₈ cup	all-purpose flour	³/₈ cup
1 tsp	ground cinnamon	1 tsp
3 tbsps	superfine sugar	75 g
	pinch salt	
3 tbsps	vegan margarine	75 g
1	large egg, beaten	1

Filling

2 tbsps	vegan margarine	50 g
¹/₂ cup	superfine sugar	110 g
1²/₃ cups	dried apricots (about ¹/₂ lb)	225 g

Soak the apricots overnight or boil for about 20 minutes until soft and then drain.

Pre-heat the oven to 375F. Grease a 10-inch-round pie pan or dish.

To make the pastry, sift the flour and cinnamon into a bowl, add the sugar and salt and mix well.

In a small pan, gently melt the margarine, stir it into the flour, mixing well, and then mix in the egg.

Press the pastry into a ball and cover in a bowl. Place in the fridge for one hour.

For the filling, melt the margarine with the sugar.

Pour into the bottom of the pie dish, covering the base.

Place the apricots over this mixture.

Roll the pastry out on a floured surface to just larger than the pie dish. Don't worry if it breaks, as you can patch it up.

Carefully lift the pastry to cover the apricots, folding over the sides if it is too big.

Pierce a couple of holes in the pastry. Cook for about 25 minutes until firm to the touch and golden.

Cool slightly, then carefully turn onto a serving plate.

PER SERVING	
Calories	295
% Calories from fat	24
Fat (g)	8.1
Saturated fat (g)	1.6
Cholesterol (mg)	26.6
Sodium (mg)	95
Protein (g)	4.3
Carbohydrate (g)	53.8
Calcium (mg)	27.8

EXCHANGES	
Milk	0.0
Vegetable	0.0
Fruit	2.0
Bread	1.5
Meat	0.0
Fat	1.5

Baked Apple Charlotte

Serves 4

The jam on the bread tends to stick slightly to the side of the dish but gives it a nice crunchy texture. The walnut oil also provides an unusual taste rather than the usual margarine.
The dish is itself quite creamy and does not really require any further cream, although my children enjoy a spoonful of soy ice cream with it.

4–5	medium cooking apples (1³/₄ lbs)	800 g
1¹/₂ tbsps	superfine sugar	37 g
5	slices stale white bread, crusts removed	5
¹/₂ cup	apricot jam	110 g
2 tbsps	walnut oil, plus extra for brushing	30 ml
1 tsp	dark brown sugar	8 g

Pre-heat the oven to 375F. Peel, core and slice the apples and put them into a heavy pan.
Add the sugar and cook, without water, until very soft. Then, using a potato masher, mash the apples until they are smooth and creamy.
Oil a 1-quart oven dish. Cut each slice of bread into 4 triangles.
Gently warm the jam with a dash of water and the walnut oil, stirring well.
Dip the pieces of bread into this jam mixture to coat each slice.
Arrange the triangles to fit the bottom and sides of the dish, saving 6 to 8 triangles for the top.
Mix any leftover jam mixture with the apple and pour into the bread-lined dish; cover with remaining bread.
Brush with extra walnut oil and sprinkle the top with dark brown sugar.
Bake for about 30 minutes until crisp and golden. Allow to cool slightly before serving.

PER SERVING	
Calories	394
% Calories from fat	19
Fat (g)	8.7
Saturated fat (g)	0.9
Cholesterol (mg)	0.3
Sodium (mg)	181
Protein (g)	3.1
Carbohydrate (g)	78.9
Calcium (mg)	56

EXCHANGES	
Milk	0.0
Vegetable	0.0
Fruit	4.5
Bread	1.0
Meat	0.0
Fat	1.5

If you do not want to use Amaretto liqueur, use a strong black espresso instead.

For anyone who wants a chocolate mousse cake, follow the recipe and stop before the final cooking stage. Pour the uncooked filling over the cookie base and refrigerate. However, this would be unsuitable for pregnant or elderly people, as the eggs would be uncooked. Delicious for anyone else.

Baked Chocolate and Almond Torte

Serves 6

This rich, slightly gooey torte turned out to be a big success with my family one cold, rainy Sunday lunch. Serve with soy cream, or be really naughty and have some soy ice cream with it.

Base		
1 tbsp	sliced almonds	1 tbsp
½ cup	crushed dairy-free cookies	110 g
2 tbsps	vegan margarine	50 g

Filling		
8 oz	dairy-free good quality dark chocolate	225 g
4	eggs, separated	4
2 tbsps	Amaretto (optional) or use dark black coffee	30 ml

Pre-heat the oven to 350F. Slightly crush the almonds and mix with the crushed cookies.

In a small pan, gently melt the margarine, pour into cookie crumbs and mix well.

Tip into a greased oven dish approximately 10 inches in diameter, and pat the mixture down flat.

Bake in the oven for about 10 minutes until firm. Allow to cool while you make the filling.

Break the chocolate into pieces and melt in a bowl over a pan of boiling water. When the chocolate is melted, remove the bowl from the pan.

In a separate bowl, beat the yolks, and while chocolate is still quite hot pour slowly over yolks, beating continuously.

Stir in the Amaretto and leave to cool.

In a large clean bowl, whisk the egg whites until they form a peak. Fold the whites into the chocolate mixture.

Pour over base, and turn oven down to 325F.

Bake for about 15 minutes, but don't overcook, as it may dry out.

The torte should be eaten when cool, and it will still be quite sticky in the middle.

PER SERVING	
Calories	348
% Calories from fat	53
Fat (g)	22.2
Saturated fat (g)	9.7
Cholesterol (mg)	146.2
Sodium (mg)	124
Protein (g)	6.6
Carbohydrate (g)	35.2
Calcium (mg)	40

EXCHANGES	
Milk	0.0
Vegetable	0.0
Fruit	0.0
Bread	2.5
Meat	0.0
Fat	4.0

Use lemons or limes for a different flavor.

Baked Orange Semolina Puddings

Serves 6

These add a new dimension to semolina. The addition of eggs makes it into a soufflé-style pudding, well worth a try. Take care not too cook these too hot and long, as they may curdle.

2–3	large juicy oranges	2–3
1 tbsp	granulated sugar	25 g
1 tbsp	semolina	1 tbsp
3	eggs, separated	3
	confectioner's sugar for dusting	

Pre-heat the oven to 375F. Grate rind and squeeze juice from 2 oranges, to make about 1 cup of juice. Use another orange if necessary.

Place orange juice, rind, sugar and semolina in a pan and simmer until thickened, stirring continuously.

Cool slightly, then stir in egg yolks.

Whisk whites until they are stiff, and fold them into the orange mixture.

Spoon into 6 lightly oiled ramekin dishes.

Bake in the oven for 15–20 minutes until risen and golden, and then dust with confectioner's sugar. Serve immediately.

PER SERVING	
Calories	70
% Calories from fat	34
Fat (g)	2.6
Saturated fat (g)	0.8
Cholesterol (mg)	106.2
Sodium (mg)	32
Protein (g)	3.6
Carbohydrate (g)	7.9
Calcium (mg)	17

EXCHANGES	
Milk	0.0
Vegetable	0.0
Fruit	0.5
Bread	0.0
Meat	0.5
Fat	0.0

Make sure the bananas are not too overripe for this recipe. For an equally delicious dessert, use fresh pineapple or apple rings.

Banana Fritters

Serves 4

Delicious crisp fritters. The addition of coconut to the batter makes the dish more exotic. Serve with soy ice cream, soy yogurt or even tofu and almond cream.

2 tbsps	all-purpose flour	2 tbsps
	pinch salt	
1	large egg	1
3/8 cup	low-fat coconut milk	90 ml
1 tbsp	superfine sugar	25 g
4	firm bananas	4
	oil for shallow frying	
1 tsp	confectioner's sugar mixed with 1 teaspoon of dried coconut	1 tsp

Sift flour with salt in a bowl. Make a well in the center. Drop in the egg and mix with a wooden spoon, gradually incorporating all the flour, then slowly add the coconut milk, stirring well. Add more coconut milk as needed to reach a thick cream consistency. Stir in the sugar and allow the batter to rest for 20 minutes.

Peel bananas, cut in half lengthways and dip into the batter.

Heat 1/4-inch-deep oil in a frying pan. When hot, fry the fritters for about 2 minutes on each side until golden brown.

Drain and dust with confectioner's sugar and coconut mix. Serve immediately while the fritters are still crisp.

PER SERVING	
Calories	171
% Calories from fat	15
Fat (g)	3.1
Saturated fat (g)	1.5
Cholesterol (mg)	53.1
Sodium (mg)	25
Protein (g)	3.2
Carbohydrate (g)	35.3
Calcium (mg)	13.5
EXCHANGES	
Milk	0.0
Vegetable	0.0
Fruit	2.5
Bread	0.0
Meat	0.0
Fat	0.5

This is also good with pears, bananas or fresh apricots.

Caramelized Apple Pie

Serves 8

This is based on the French "Tarte Tatin" recipe. I have included it as it is a super-fast recipe for anyone wanting to produce a quick dessert for their lactose-free guests. Serve with soy yogurt, soy ice cream or Tofu and Almond Cream (page 170).

2 tbsps	dark brown sugar	50 g
1 tbsp	walnut oil	15 ml
1 tsp	ground cinnamon	1 tsp
3–4	medium apples, peeled, cored and very thinly sliced (about 1 lb.)	450 g
1/2 lb	puff pastry, shop bought	225 g

Pre-heat the oven to 400F. Oil a 10-inch round oven dish, which is at least 3/4 inch high. Sprinkle sugar on the bottom of dish and drizzle over oil and cinnamon.

Lay apples in a neat circle over the sugar, ensuring that all the base is covered. If necessary, layer more apples on top.

Roll out pastry and cut into a circle about 3/4 inch larger than the round base. Cover the apples with the pastry, pressing it down gently; fold the edges back over.

Bake in the oven for 20–25 minutes until well risen, crisp and golden.

Turn out onto a warm plate to serve.

PER SERVING	
Calories	218
% Calories from fat	51
Fat (g)	12.7
Saturated fat (g)	2.9
Cholesterol (mg)	0
Sodium (mg)	72
Protein (g)	2.2
Carbohydrate (g)	25
Calcium (mg)	13.3

EXCHANGES	
Milk	0.0
Vegetable	0.0
Fruit	1.0
Bread	1.0
Meat	0.0
Fat	2.0

If you don't have whiskey, use a brandy or liqueur; otherwise soak the prunes in orange juice.
  Try using coconut milk instead of soy cream for a more exotic pudding.

Chocolate, Prune and Whiskey Bread Pudding

Serves 6

This is a good dinner party dessert, and your friends will not believe it is lactose-free. It is also a great way of using up any excess bread. Prunes not only increase the nutritional value of the dish but also make a wonderful combination with chocolate. Serve with soy cream or soy ice cream.

1/3 cup	pitted prunes, cut into 4 pieces	1/3 cup
2 tbsps	whiskey	30 ml
6	slices of thick-sliced white bread	6
1 tbsp	vegan margarine	25 g
3 oz	dark dairy-free chocolate, cut into small pieces	85 g
1 tbsp	cocoa powder	1 tbsp
1 1/8 cups	soy milk	270 ml
3 tbsps	superfine sugar	75 g
3	eggs	3
6 tbsps	soy cream	90 ml
	sprinkling of crystallized sugar, optional	

Pre-heat the oven to 350F. You will need an oven-proof dish with a base measurement of about 8 x 6 inches, 1 1/2 inches deep, lightly greased.

About 2 hours before you start, pour whiskey over the prunes in a small bowl and leave to soak.

Remove the crusts from the bread and lightly spread the slices with margarine. Cut each slice of bread into 4 squares, and lay half over the bottom of the oven-proof dish.

Cover with the prunes, whiskey and chocolate chunks, then place the remaining bread over the top, overlapping slightly, margarine side up.

Sieve the cocoa in a medium mixing bowl and gradually add the soy milk, making sure cocoa is mixed in thoroughly. Beat in the eggs, sugar and soy cream.

Pour this cocoa mixture over the bread. Press the top gently with a fork to ensure all the bread is coated.

Sprinkle on a little crystallized sugar.

Bake for 30–40 minutes. The pudding will rise slightly, and the surface should be crisp and golden.

PER SERVING	
Calories	283
% Calories from fat	37
Fat (g)	12
Saturated fat (g)	4.2
Cholesterol (mg)	107.6
Sodium (mg)	199
Protein (g)	7.4
Carbohydrate (g)	35.6
Calcium (mg)	51.2

EXCHANGES	
Milk	0.0
Vegetable	0.0
Fruit	0.5
Bread	2.0
Meat	0.0
Fat	2.5

Coconut contains a high proportion of saturated fats. It is a good addition to the vegetarian dairy-free diet, although those with a meat-centered diet should limit their intake.

Coconut Crème Caramel

Serves 4

When I tried to make a crème caramel with soy milk, the result was very watery and not particularly successful. Made with coconut milk, however, the result was a creamy light custard with a delicate coconut flavor.

3/4 cup	superfine sugar	170 g
1	14-oz can reduced-fat coconut milk	1
3	medium eggs	3

Pre-heat the oven to 300F. Put half of the sugar in a heavy pan over low heat.

Stir and let the sugar caramelize. When melted and golden brown (not burnt), pour the caramel equally into 4 ramekins.

In a small pan, heat the coconut milk over low heat until warm.

In a bowl, beat the eggs with the remaining sugar until light and creamy.

Gradually add the coconut milk, beating as you do so.

Strain the custard and pour into ramekins. Put the ramekins in a baking pan, and pour enough hot water around them so it comes halfway up the cups.

Bake for 30–40 minutes, until the coconut caramels are set. When cool, refrigerate in the ramekins.

To serve, run a knife around the edges of the bowls and invert onto plates. Makes 4 individual custards.

PER SERVING	
Calories	259
% Calories from fat	31
Fat (g)	9.1
Saturated fat (g)	4.7
Cholesterol (mg)	159.4
Sodium (mg)	87
Protein (g)	4.7
Carbohydrate (g)	40
Calcium (mg)	18.7

EXCHANGES	
Milk	0.0
Vegetable	0.0
Fruit	0.0
Bread	2.5
Meat	0.0
Fat	2.0

Note that any liqueur can be used, such as Amaretto or a chocolate liqueur (as long as it contains no cream).

Coffee Zabaglione

Serves 4

This pudding is surprisingly creamy and light and is excellent served warm with a crisp cookie. This dish can also be frozen and served as zabaglione ice cream.

4	egg yolks	4
2 tbsps	superfine sugar	50 g
¼ cup	strong black coffee	60 ml
2 tbsps	coffee liqueur (such as Tia Maria)	30 ml
	cocoa powder for decoration	

Combine egg yolks and sugar in a bowl. Whisk for several minutes with an electric beater until pale and frothy. Transfer to top of double boiler.

Over simmering water, gradually beat in half the coffee and half the liqueur.

Beat constantly for about 10 minutes over heat until thick and creamy.

Then whisk in the remaining coffee and liqueur. If the mixture adheres to side of pan, quickly remove from heat and beat vigorously with wooden spoon, especially around base.

Pour into individual dishes.

Sprinkle with cocoa powder before serving.

PER SERVING	
Calories	112
% Calories from fat	41
Fat (g)	5.2
Saturated fat (g)	1.6
Cholesterol (mg)	212.6
Sodium (mg)	8
Protein (g)	2.8
Carbohydrate (g)	10.4
Calcium (mg)	23.2
EXCHANGES	
Milk	0.0
Vegetable	0.0
Fruit	0.0
Bread	1.0
Meat	0.0
Fat	1.0

When making flans or tarts, metal pans are preferable, as they conduct heat better; the result will be a crisper pastry shell. The filling could also be made using any ripe seasonal fruit such as strawberries, black currants, blackberries, peaches or nectarines. Or why not try it with a mixture of berries?

Fresh Raspberry Tart

Serves 8

This is a lovely summer dessert. It can be finished an hour or so before serving and refrigerated. The sweet pastry base retains its crispiness well.

1 recipe	Crisp Sweet Pastry (page 186)	1 recipe
1 recipe	Pastry Cream (page 165)	1 recipe
3 cups	firm ripe raspberries (about 1 lb)	450 g
1 tbsp	red currant jelly (or any other fruit jelly) to glaze	1 tbsp

Pre-heat the oven to 400F. On a floured surface, roll out the pastry thinly and line a greased pie pan approximately 9 inches in diameter and 2 inches deep, with fluted edges. Trim the pastry to fit pan and prick the base.

Fill with waxed paper and dried beans and bake blind for about 10 minutes.

Remove beans and paper and reduce oven temperature to 350F. Return to oven for about 7 minutes to dry out.

Remove from the oven and allow to cool.

Fill the pastry case with cooled pastry cream, smoothing down well.

Arrange the raspberries on top to cover completely; it doesn't matter if they overlap slightly.

Mix the jelly with a fork to let it loosen slightly (if necessary, warm slightly) and brush over the tart to cover the raspberries completely.

Refrigerate before serving.

PER SERVING	
Calories	196
% Calories from fat	39
Fat (g)	8.7
Saturated fat (g)	1.9
Cholesterol (mg)	132.9
Sodium (mg)	60
Protein (g)	4.3
Carbohydrate (g)	25.7
Calcium (mg)	29.3
EXCHANGES	
Milk	0.0
Vegetable	0.0
Fruit	1.0
Bread	1.0
Meat	0.0
Fat	1.0

For the non-alcoholic version, substitute extra orange juice for the Amaretto.

Honey-Glazed Pineapple and Fig Kebabs with Orange Sabayon

Serves 4

This is a relatively healthy dessert that leaves you feeling like you've had something wicked! For those not so keen on a sabayon-style sauce, the kebabs would be great with soy ice cream or, if you feel very virtuous, Oat and Honey Cream (see page 169).

Kebabs

¹/₂	medium, ripe pineapple	¹/₂
3	ripe figs, quartered	3
2 tbsps	honey	2 tbsps
4	long skewers	4

Sabayon

3	egg yolks	3
1 tbsp	superfine sugar	25 g
¹/₄ cup	orange juice	60 ml
	zest of one orange	
2 tbsps	Amaretto (optional)	30 ml

Peel the pineapple and remove any brown bits. Remove core and cut into 16 equal-sized cubes.

Alternate pieces of pineapple and fig so you have 4 pieces of pineapple and 3 pieces of fig on each skewer. Spoon over and cover well with the runny honey, and place skewers in an oven-proof dish.

Pre-heat broiler. Broil for about 3 minutes, turn skewer and broil 3 minutes on the other side. Fruit should be beginning to caramelize.

For the Sabayon: put all the ingredients in a double-boiler and simmer. Whisk until light and fluffy, about 5 minutes.

Serve immediately with the grilled kebabs.

PER SERVING	
Calories	155
% Calories from fat	23
Fat (g)	4.2
Saturated fat (g)	1.2
Cholesterol (mg)	159.5
Sodium (mg)	7
Protein (g)	2.8
Carbohydrate (g)	28.7
Calcium (mg)	41.5

EXCHANGES	
Milk	0.0
Vegetable	0.0
Fruit	2.0
Bread	0.0
Meat	0.0
Fat	1.0

Vary the fruit in this crumble according to availability. For example, use black currants or blackberries.

Mixed Berry and Peach Coconut Crumble

Serves 4

Crumbles are simple to make and a wonderful way of using seasonal fresh fruit. The topping for this crumble has the unusual addition of coconut, oats and almonds, which complement the hot fruit perfectly. Serve with soy ice cream, soy yogurt or soy custard.

½ cup	blueberries	110 g
½ cup	raspberries	110 g
2	fresh peaches	2
3½ fl oz	black currant cordial or black currant syrup	105 ml

Topping

2 tbsps	all-purpose flour	2 tbsps
2 tbsps	ground almonds	2 tbsps
2 tbsps	vegan margarine	50 g
2 tbsps	dried coconut	2 tbsps
1 tbsp	superfine sugar	25 g
1 tbsp	quick-cooking oats	25 g

Pre-heat the oven to 350F. You will need a 1-quart oven dish. Remove the stones from the peaches and cut flesh into small chunks.

Arrange the berries and peaches in the oven dish. Pour over the cordial. Alternatively, you could use elderberry cordial.

For the topping, put the flour and almonds in a bowl and rub in the margarine until the mixture resembles breadcrumbs.

Stir in the coconut, sugar and oats. Spread evenly over the top of the fruit.

Bake in oven for about 30 minutes, until the top is golden.

PER SERVING	
Calories	256
% Calories from fat	30
Fat (g)	8.9
Saturated fat (g)	2
Cholesterol (mg)	0
Sodium (mg)	71
Protein (g)	2.2
Carbohydrate (g)	32.7
Calcium (mg)	21
EXCHANGES	
Milk	0.0
Vegetable	0.0
Fruit	1.0
Bread	1.0
Meat	0.0
Fat	2.5

Pears could be substituted for with pineapple or apples.

Pear and Ginger Upside Down Cake

Serves 6

This is a favorite dessert of mine that keeps well and may be easily reheated. It is also nice eaten cold. Serve hot with soy ice cream, soy cream or soy custard.

2 tbsps	vegan margarine	50 g
3 tbsps	superfine sugar	75 g
2–3	large, firm but ripe pears, peeled, cored and cut into eighths	2–3
2	eggs, beaten	2
2 tbsps	molasses	2 tbsps
3 tbsps	vegan margarine, melted	75 g
2/3 cup	superfine sugar	150 g
3 tbsps	crystallized ginger, roughly chopped	3 tbsps
3 1/2 fl oz	soy milk	105 ml
2 tsps	ground ginger	2 tsps
1/2 tsp	ground cinnamon	1/2 tsp
3/4 cup	self-rising flour	3/4 cup

Pre-heat the oven to 350F. Grease a circular 10-inch-diameter, 2-inch-deep oven dish.

To make the topping, cream together the margarine and sugar.

Smear this mixture over the base of the dish and lay the pears neatly in a circle, tips touching, in the center of the dish.

Beat together the eggs, molasses, melted margarine, sugar, crystallized ginger and soy milk.

Sift the spices and flour into the egg mixture and mix thoroughly.

Pour over the pears, smooth down and bake for about 40 minutes until cooked through.

Leave for a few minutes, then, using a knife, go around the edge of the dish. Turn out onto a warm plate. Serve hot.

PER SERVING	
Calories	367
% Calories from fat	28
Fat (g)	11.9
Saturated fat (g)	2.5
Cholesterol (mg)	70.8
Sodium (mg)	338
Protein (g)	4.5
Carbohydrate (g)	62.8
Calcium (mg)	88.3

EXCHANGES	
Milk	0.0
Vegetable	0.0
Fruit	0.0
Bread	4.0
Meat	0.0
Fat	2.0

Egg yolks were used to increase the protein content of the pudding. However, if you are cooking for a vegan omit the egg yolks and the pudding will still be delicious.

Raisin, Lemon and Almond Rice Pudding

Serves 4

This is a tasty, nursery-style pudding that kids will love. The raisins swell up and become really juicy, giving the pudding added natural sweetness. I added the almonds to provide a creamy texture as well as increase the calcium content.

2 cups	vanilla rice milk	480 ml
2 tbsps	ground rice powder	2 tbsps
2 tbsps	raisins	2 tbsps
1 tbsp	ground almonds	1 tbsp
1 tsp	vanilla extract	1 tsp
2 tsps	honey	2 tsps
1	large lemon, grated zest only	1
2	egg yolks	2

In a large saucepan, whisk the rice milk slowly into the ground rice powder until smooth.

Add the raisins and ground almonds.

Cook over medium heat until the mixture thickens. Reduce the heat and simmer for about 6 minutes, stirring occasionally.

Stir in the vanilla, honey and grated rind, and remove from heat. Allow to cool slightly (about 5 minutes).

Beat in the egg yolks, return to heat and cook gently for about 5 minutes, taking care not to boil and curdle the yolks.

Serve hot in individual bowls.

PER SERVING	
Calories	192
% Calories from fat	31
Fat (g)	6.9
Saturated fat (g)	1.3
Cholesterol (mg)	106.3
Sodium (mg)	205
Protein (g)	23
Carbohydrate (g)	31.4
Calcium (mg)	421.7
EXCHANGES	
Milk	0.0
Vegetable	0.0
Fruit	0.0
Bread	2.0
Meat	0.0
Fat	1.0

Also delicious with gooseberries, apples, plums or fresh apricots, whatever is in season.

Tip: metal pans help make the pastry crisp.

Rhubarb and Almond Tart

Serves 8

This is an easy tart to prepare, as the pastry does not require pre-cooking. The tart is filled with an almond mixture with the uncooked rhubarb laid on top. It may be left in the fridge at this stage and put in the oven an hour before serving. Serve warm with soy cream or soy ice cream.

1 recipe	Shortcrust Pastry (see page 187)	1 recipe
2 tbsps	raspberry jam	2 tbsps
1/2 cup	vegan margarine	110 g
1/2 cup	brown sugar	110 g
2	eggs, beaten	2
1	orange	1
1/2 cup	ground almonds	1/2 cup
1 tbsp	all-purpose flour	1 tbsp
1 bunch	rhubarb, cut into 1/2-inch pieces (about 3/4 lb)	337 g
	red currant jelly for glazing	

Pre-heat the oven to 350F. On a floured surface, roll the pastry out thinly and line a greased 9-inch pie pan.

Prick base with a fork and smear over the jam.

In a medium bowl, beat the margarine and sugar until light and creamy, then gradually add the eggs and beat well. Grate in the zest from the orange, and squeeze the juice of half. Stir in the almonds and flour.

When well blended, pour into the pie pan and smooth down.

Arrange the rhubarb neatly over the top, pushing down slightly into the almond mixture, but not completely submerging.

Bake in the oven for 40–50 minutes until firm to the touch and golden.

Glaze with jelly. Serve warm or chilled.

PER SERVING	
Calories	360
% Calories from fat	56
Fat (g)	23
Saturated fat (g)	4.8
Cholesterol (mg)	56.1
Sodium (mg)	191
Protein (g)	5.6
Carbohydrate (g)	34.5
Calcium (mg)	88.6
EXCHANGES	
Milk	0.0
Vegetable	0.0
Fruit	0.5
Bread	2.0
Meat	0.0
Fat	4.0

Cut into smaller squares and serve for a picnic or buffet.

Chocolate Brownies

Serves 16 (1 per serving)

Serve with chocolate sauce and vanilla soy ice cream for a very indulgent yummy pudding. Alternatively, serve cold as an anytime treat. Store in an airtight container for up to 6 days.

10 oz	dark dairy-free chocolate	280 g
1 cup	vegan margarine	220 g
1 1/8 cups	brown sugar	247 g
4	eggs, beaten	4
1 tsp	vanilla extract	1 tsp
1/2 cup	self-rising flour	1/2 cup
1/2 tsp	baking soda	1/2 tsp
	pinch salt	
1 tbsp	cocoa powder	1 tbsp
3/4 cup	chopped hazelnuts	3/4 cup

Pre-heat the oven to 325F. Line the base of a baking pan approximately 8 x 12 inches and 2 inches deep with waxed paper.

Put the chocolate in a double-boiler, and stir until melted.

Cream the margarine and sugar by hand or in a food processor until well blended.

Gradually add the eggs and vanilla extract, mixing well.

Pour in the chocolate slowly, beating constantly.

Sieve together the flour, baking soda, salt and cocoa.

Fold the flour and chopped hazelnuts into the chocolate mixture until well combined.

Pour into the lined baking pan and smooth down. Bake on the center shelf for 35–40 minutes.

Brownies should be firm and slightly dry around the edges, and a toothpick should come out almost clean when put into the confection.

Cut into 16 squares and serve warm.

PER SERVING	
Calories	323
% Calories from fat	60
Fat (g)	22.5
Saturated fat (g)	6.4
Cholesterol (mg)	54.5
Sodium (mg)	244
Protein (g)	3.7
Carbohydrate (g)	30.4
Calcium (mg)	49.7
EXCHANGES	
Milk	0.0
Vegetable	0.0
Fruit	0.0
Bread	2.0
Meat	0.0
Fat	4.0

For a differently flavored cheesecake, try using other fruit purées such as raspberry or strawberry.

Tangy Citrus Cheesecake

Serves 8

This is an extremely successful dessert. The addition of tofu and cashew nuts not only makes it quite nutritious but contributes to the creamy cheesecake texture. Serve decorated with seasonal fresh berries or Fresh Raspberry Coulis (see page 166). For a vegan cheesecake, use Jello instead of gelatin, following the manufacturer's instructions.

Base

6 oz	vanilla wafers (check that they are lactose free)	170 g
3 tbsps	vegan margarine	75 g

Filling

1	lime	1
1	lemon	1
1–2	oranges	1–2
3 tbsps	cashew nuts	3 tbsps
½ cup	firm tofu (about 4 oz)	112 g
½ cup	soy milk	120 ml
2 tbsps	superfine sugar	50 g
1	envelope gelatin (¼ oz)	1

To make the base: crush the cookies to fine crumbs. Melt margarine in small pan, taking care not to overheat.

Stir the melted margarine into the cookie crumbs, mixing well.

Press into a lightly oiled 8-inch springform cake pan. Refrigerate to harden.

For the filling: grate the zest from all the fruit.

Squeeze the lime, lemon and oranges until there is about 1 cup of juice altogether.

In a liquidizer or food processor, blend the cashew nuts, tofu, soy milk and sugar until it becomes smooth and silky.

Reserving 4 tablespoons of citrus juice to one side, pour remaining juice into the food processor and continue processing.

Soak the gelatin in a bowl of cold water until it becomes soft. Heat the reserved citrus juice until warm, add softened gelatin, and melt over warm heat until dissolved.

Pour the melted gelatin into the cheesecake mixture, stirring well. Pour the filling over the base and allow to set in the fridge. Serve chilled.

PER SERVING	
Calories	207
% Calories from fat	50
Fat (g)	11.6
Saturated fat (g)	2.6
Cholesterol (mg)	0
Sodium (mg)	137
Protein (g)	3.9
Carbohydrate (g)	22.6
Calcium (mg)	39.3

EXCHANGES	
Milk	0.0
Vegetable	0.0
Fruit	0.0
Bread	1.5
Meat	0.0
Fat	2.0

If the sauce solidifies when cold, reheat slowly to sauce consistency.

Chocolate Fudge Sauce

Serves 8 (2 tablespoons per serving)

This sauce is easy to do with a result that is as good as any chocolate fudge sauce made using butter. Perfect for serving warm or cold as an accompaniment to ice creams or sponge cakes.

2 oz	dark dairy-free chocolate	56 g
½ cup	dark brown sugar	110 g
1 tbsp	cocoa powder, sifted	1 tbsp
2 tsps	vanilla extract	2 tsps

Place all the ingredients in a saucepan, along with 1 cup cold water. Slowly bring to a boil, stirring occasionally.

Boil for 2–3 minutes, stirring constantly, and remove from heat. Serve hot. Makes about 1 cup.

PER SERVING	
Calories	93
% Calories from fat	22
Fat (g)	2.4
Saturated fat (g)	1.4
Cholesterol (mg)	0.5
Sodium (mg)	6
Protein (g)	0.4
Carbohydrate (g)	18.2
Calcium (mg)	14.1
EXCHANGES	
Milk	0.0
Vegetable	0.0
Fruit	0.0
Bread	1.0
Meat	0.0
Fat	0.5

This confection can also be flavored with cocoa to make a delicious chocolate filling.

Another idea is to mix this with fruit purées such as apple and blackberry and pour into individual parfait glasses as a tasty pudding. Try this for your children.

Pastry Cream

Serves 6 (about 2¹/₂ tablespoons per serving)

Crème Pâtissière, or Pastry Cream, is the delicious custard-like filling used in many French tarts. It can be used as a creamy filling for many desserts and is excellent served with stewed fruit. I use it to fill a Fresh Raspberry Tart (see page 156).

1 cup	soy milk	240 ml
2	large egg yolks	2
2 tbsps	superfine sugar	50 g
³/₄ tbsp	all-purpose flour	³/₄ tbsp
³/₄ tbsp	cornstarch	³/₄ tbsp
¹/₂ tsp	vanilla extract	¹/₂ tsp
2 tbsps	soy cream	30 ml

In a medium saucepan, heat the soy milk until fairly hot but not boiling.

In a medium bowl, cream the yolks and sugar until pale, then whisk in the sieved flour and cornstarch.

Gradually pour in the milk and stir well. Return the mixture to the milk pan.

Slowly bring up to a boil, stirring continuously. It will begin to go thick and lumpy, but just stir well until smooth.

Allow to cool slightly, then add the vanilla and soy cream.

Use chilled as required. Makes 1 cup.

PER SERVING	
Calories	62
% Calories from fat	41
Fat (g)	2.8
Saturated fat (g)	0.6
Cholesterol (mg)	70.9
Sodium (mg)	9
Protein (g)	2.1
Carbohydrate (g)	6.9
Calcium (mg)	9.4
EXCHANGES	
Milk	0.0
Vegetable	0.0
Fruit	0.0
Bread	0.5
Meat	0.0
Fat	0.5

Tip: If you are not serving the custard immediately, lay waxed paper over to cover the top, and this will prevent a skin from forming.

PER SERVING	
Calories	119
% Calories from fat	36
Fat (g)	4.9
Saturated fat (g)	1.1
Cholesterol (mg)	106.3
Sodium (mg)	18
Protein (g)	4.7
Carbohydrate (g)	14.4
Calcium (mg)	16.4
EXCHANGES	
Milk	0.0
Vegetable	0.0
Fruit	0.0
Bread	1.0
Meat	0.0
Fat	1.0

This can be made using fresh strawberries or black currants.

PER SERVING	
Calories	45
% Calories from fat	6
Fat (g)	0.3
Saturated fat (g)	0
Cholesterol (mg)	0
Sodium (mg)	0
Protein (g)	0.6
Carbohydrate (g)	10.8
Calcium (mg)	13.6
EXCHANGES	
Milk	0.0
Vegetable	0.0
Fruit	1.0
Bread	0.0
Meat	0.0
Fat	0.0

Custard Sauce

Serves 4 ($^1/_2$ cup per serving)

In my household, custard has to be the number one favorite, especially with hot puddings. The yolks give the custard a higher protein content and also add creaminess.

2 cups	soy milk	480 ml
2	egg yolks	2
1 tsp	vanilla extract or fresh vanilla pod	1 tsp
$^1/_4$ cup	sugar or to taste	55 g

Warm the soy milk over medium heat, taking care not to let it boil.

In a bowl, mix the egg yolks and vanilla essence. Next, pour the warm milk over the mixture, beating well.

Return to the pan and stir over low heat until it thickens, taking care not to cook too quickly and curdle the eggs.

Sweeten with sugar to taste. Serve hot. Makes just over 2 cups.

Fresh Raspberry Coulis

Serves 4–6 (about $^1/_2$ cup per serving)

Serve with soy ice creams, fresh fruit pies, cheesecakes or even fresh fruit salad.

2 cups	fresh raspberries or frozen (about 11 oz)	310 g
2–3 tbsps	confectioner's sugar	2–3 tbsps

Defrost the raspberries if frozen. Push the fruit through a sieve to remove seeds.

Sift in the confectioner's sugar and mix well.

Taste for sweetness and add more sugar if necessary.

If the coulis is too thick, dilute with water or apple juice. Makes about 2 cups.

Rich Butterscotch Sauce

Serves 8 (2 tablespoons per serving)

Butterscotch sauce would usually be made with condensed milk, but this version using coconut milk works very well and is almost as delicious. Serve with soy ice cream, bananas, meringues or sponge cake or even try it with pineapple, banana or apple fritters.

1 cup	(scant) water	220 ml
1/2 cup	dark brown sugar	110 g
1 cup	(scant) reduced-fat coconut milk	220 ml
1/2 tbsp	arrowroot	1/2 tbsp

Place the water and sugar in a small saucepan over low heat. Stir until dissolved, then bring to a boil and simmer for 15 minutes.

Remove from heat and leave for several minutes; add coconut milk and stir well.

Mix arrowroot with a tablespoon of water until smooth.

Pour the arrowroot into the sauce and stir over gentle heat to thicken slightly.

Serve hot or cold. Makes just over 1 cup.

PER SERVING	
Calories	70
% Calories from fat	19
Fat (g)	1.5
Saturated fat (g)	1
Cholesterol (mg)	0
Sodium (mg)	16
Protein (g)	0
Carbohydrate (g)	14.4
Calcium (mg)	11.7

EXCHANGES	
Milk	0.0
Vegetable	0.0
Fruit	0.0
Bread	1.0
Meat	0.0
Fat	0.0

Try making this sauce with coconut milk instead of the soy cream.

Mocha Chocolate Sauce

Serves 8 (2 tablespoons per serving)

This rich chocolate and coffee sauce is perfect served hot with chocolate brownies, soy ice cream and many puddings.

5 oz	dark dairy-free chocolate, broken into chunks	140 g
2/3 cup	strong hot espresso coffee	150 ml
2/3 cup	soy cream	150 ml

Put the chocolate chunks into the top of a double-boiler over boiling water.

Melt the chocolate and stir until smooth. When thoroughly melted, remove from the heat.

Slowly pour some of the hot coffee into the chocolate, stirring gently. Initially the chocolate will appear to go thick and solid. Do not worry, but just continue stirring and adding hot coffee slowly. Eventually it will become smooth and silky.

Finally, add the soy cream and mix well. The result should be a smooth-pouring chocolate sauce.

This can be allowed to cool and then reheated either in a microwave or over a pan of boiling water.

Serve hot. Makes about 1 cup.

PER SERVING	
Calories	109
% Calories from fat	56
Fat (g)	7.3
Saturated fat (g)	3.5
Cholesterol (mg)	1.4
Sodium (mg)	7
Protein (g)	0.7
Carbohydrate (g)	12.3
Calcium (mg)	6.1
EXCHANGES	
Milk	0.0
Vegetable	0.0
Fruit	0.0
Bread	1.0
Meat	0.0
Fat	1.0

For a better result, use fine oatmeal rather than large oats.

Oat and Honey Cream

Serves 6 (¹/₄ cup per serving)

This cream has a lovely consistency. However, the cream will have a slightly grainy taste because the oats have been broken down during the processing. This does make it very nutritious, as hardly any parts of the oats have been removed.

Serve as very low-fat cream with hot puddings. Delicious with stewed fruits such as pear and apple or even a warm apple pie. Use in the Banana Oat Shake on page 192.

3 tbsps	quick-cooking oats	75 g
1¹/₂ cups	(scant) cold water (use more water for a thinner cream)	340 ml
2 tbsps	honey	2 tbsps

Soak the oats in the water and honey for at least 2 hours. Blend in a food processor or liquidizer until smooth.

Sieve well and refrigerate until required.

This will keep well in the fridge for several days. Makes about 1¹/₂ cups.

PER SERVING	
Calories	31
% Calories from fat	5
Fat (g)	0.2
Saturated fat (g)	0
Cholesterol (mg)	0
Sodium (mg)	0
Protein (g)	0.4
Carbohydrate (g)	7.5
Calcium (mg)	1.6

EXCHANGES	
Milk	0.0
Vegetable	0.0
Fruit	0.0
Bread	0.5
Meat	0.0
Fat	0.0

To make an alternative to sour cream, omit the vanilla and honey, and squeeze in a dash of lemon juice. Cashew nuts can also be used to produce a cream equally as delicious.

Once you start experimenting with this, many variations are possible by adding more nuts and less tofu, etc.

Tofu and Almond Cream

Serves 4 (¹/₄ cup per serving)

This makes a useful sauce to serve in place of dairy products such as cream, yogurt and ice cream. Based on tofu and almonds, it is more nutritious and fairly low in fat compared to many creams.

2 tbsps	soy milk	30 ml
¹/₂ cup	firm tofu (about 4 oz)	112 g
2 tbsps	blanched almonds (sliced, ground or whole)	2 tbsps
1 inch	vanilla pod (or 1 teaspoon vanilla extract)	2.5 cm
1 tsp	honey (more depending on taste)	1 tsp

Use a blender or food processor to blend all the ingredients, except honey, until smooth and creamy.

Add honey to taste, and blend again to mix well.

Refrigerate until required. This cream will last several days in the fridge. Makes about 1 cup.

PER SERVING	
Calories	62
% Calories from fat	53
Fat (g)	3.8
Saturated fat (g)	0.3
Cholesterol (mg)	0
Sodium (mg)	2
Protein (g)	3.7
Carbohydrate (g)	3.2
Calcium (mg)	57
EXCHANGES	
Milk	0.0
Vegetable	0.0
Fruit	0.0
Bread	0.0
Meat	0.5
Fat	0.5

Baking, Breakfasts and Beverages

Bacon, Onion and Sage Scones

Onion, Tomato and Rosemary Focaccia

Seedy Muffins

Polenta Bread Rolls

Carrot and Raisin Cake with Lemon and Orange Frosting

Chocolate and Almond Pithiviers

Coconut and Chocolate Oat Cakes

Raisin and Peanut Cookies

Fresh Strawberry Cake Roll

Orange and Almond Shortbread

Spiced Apple and Walnut Cake

Wicked Chocolate Cake

Cornmeal Pastry

Crisp Sweet Pastry

Quick Flaky Pastry

Shortcrust Pastry

Whole Wheat Pastry

Blueberry Muffins

Corn Griddle Cakes

Kedgeree

French Toast

Banana Oat Shake

Summer Berry Fruit Crush

These can be made with ham or pastrami for a slightly different flavor. Vegetarians should omit the bacon.

Bacon, Onion and Sage Scones

Serves 12 (1 scone per serving)

If I have run out of bread, I often make scones, as they take so little time to prepare and bake. These scones are particularly good served hot from the oven with a steaming bowl of homemade soup. They are also delicious cold as a sandwich with soy cream cheese and watercress or baby spinach for a picnic or packed lunch.

1 tbsp	olive oil	15 ml
1	medium onion, finely chopped	1
5–6 slices	smoked bacon, finely chopped (4 oz)	112 g
1¼ cups	self-rising flour	1¼ cups
	pinch salt	
1 tbsp	vegan margarine	25 g
8	sage leaves, chopped	8
1 cup	soy milk	240 ml

Grease 2 large baking sheets. Pre-heat the oven to 425F.

In a frying pan, heat the oil and sauté the onions for 5 minutes. Add the bacon and continue cooking for several minutes until cooked through.

Sift the flour and salt into a large mixing bowl. Lightly rub in the margarine until the mixture resembles breadcrumbs.

Stir the onion and bacon mixture, sage and soy milk into the flour to form sticky dough.

Turn out onto floured surface.

Knead gently until smooth, then roll the dough out to 1 inch thick, and stamp into small rounds.

Place scones on the prepared baking sheets.

Bake in the oven for about 15 minutes or until well-risen and golden brown.

Leave to cool on a wire rack, or serve hot from the oven. Makes 12.

PER SERVING	
Calories	94
% Calories from fat	41
Fat (g)	4.3
Saturated fat (g)	1
Cholesterol (mg)	2.8
Sodium (mg)	232
Protein (g)	3
Carbohydrate (g)	10.9
Calcium (mg)	49.8
EXCHANGES	
Milk	0.0
Vegetable	0.0
Fruit	0.0
Bread	1.0
Meat	0.0
Fat	0.5

Try other versions using fresh chopped basil and black olives.
  Active dry yeast makes baking quicker and simpler. Unlike some ordinary dried yeasts, it does not need sugar or pre-mixing with warm water. If you wish to use ordinary dried yeast or fresh yeast, you will need to follow the manufacturer's instructions.

Onion, Tomato and Rosemary Focaccia

Serves 6–8

The combination of the caramelized onions, sun-dried tomatoes and rosemary gives this bread a wonderful flavor, particularly when still fresh from the oven. Serve with hot homemade soup or as part of a barbecue or buffet. I also recommend you try serving it with Sicilian Caponata (see page 108) to make an unusual starter or light meal.

2	medium onions, halved and thinly sliced	2
4 tbsps	olive oil	60 ml
3⅓ cups	bread flour	3⅓ cups
2 tsp	fine salt	2 tsp
1	¼-oz packet active dry yeast	1
1¾ cups	lukewarm water	420 ml
½ cup	sun-dried tomatoes packed in oil, drained and chopped	½ cup
	large sprig of fresh rosemary, stalks removed and leaves chopped	
1 tsp	coarse salt	1 tsp

Grease a large baking sheet. Sauté the onions in 1 tablespoon of olive oil over medium heat for about 8 minutes until tender but not too soft.

Sieve the flour and fine salt into a bowl, then stir in the yeast. Next, pour in 2 tablespoons of the olive oil, and then gradually work in the water a little at a time until you have a manageable, soft dough that is not too sticky. You may not need all the water.

Tip the dough out onto a floured surface and knead for about 8 minutes until you have a silky dough.

Work in the chopped sun-dried tomatoes and chopped rosemary, and continue kneading until they are all well incorporated.

Work the dough into a large flat circle about 14 inches in diameter.

Lay the dough on the prepared baking sheet, then, using your fingers, poke lots of holes over the top, cover with onions and drizzle with remaining 1 tablespoon of olive oil and sprinkle over the rock salt.

Leave in a warm place to rise slowly for about 45 minutes, until doubled in size.

PER SERVING	
Calories	393
% Calories from fat	27
Fat (g)	11.7
Saturated fat (g)	1.6
Cholesterol (mg)	0
Sodium (mg)	1191
Protein (g)	10.5
Carbohydrate (g)	61.2
Calcium (mg)	29

EXCHANGES	
Milk	0.0
Vegetable	0.0
Fruit	0.0
Bread	4.0
Meat	0.0
Fat	2.0

While the dough is rising, pre-heat the oven to 425F.

Bake in the oven for 15 minutes; check and turn tray around if the focaccia is cooking unevenly. Bake for further 7–8 minutes, until risen and golden brown with crisp, darkening onions.

Lift the focaccia off the tray onto a cooling rack. Serve warm or at room temperature.

Store for several days in an airtight container. When using seeds, check that they are fresh, as the essential oils can quickly become rancid. For a fruity muffin, use raisins and chopped apple.

Seedy Muffins

Serves 9 (1 muffin per serving)

Seeds and malted wheat give an excellent texture and provide valuable vitamins and minerals. These muffins are fairly quick and easy to prepare and can be served either sweet with fruit jams or honey or savory with soy cream cheese and slices of ham, bacon, gravlax or smoked salmon.

3 tbsps	all-purpose flour	3 tbsps
1/2 cup	whole-wheat flour	1/2 cup
1 1/2 tsps	baking powder	1 1/2 tsps
2 tbsps	brown sugar	50 g
1/2 tsp	salt	1/2 tsp
1 tbsp	sunflower seeds	1 tbsp
1 tbsp	sesame seeds	1 tbsp
1 tbsp	pumpkin seeds	1 tbsp
2	eggs	2
1/2 cup	rice milk	120 ml
1 tbsp	sunflower oil	15 ml
1 tbsp	malt extract	1 tbsp

Pre-heat the oven to 400F. Grease a 9-hole muffin pan or place 9 paper muffin cup cases on a baking sheet.

In a large bowl, combine the flours and baking powder, brown sugar, salt and seeds, mixing well.

In a separate bowl, beat the eggs, then whisk in the rice milk, sunflower oil and malt extract until well blended.

Pour this liquid over the dry ingredients and stir thoroughly. The mixture should have the consistency of a thick batter. Add more rice milk if necessary. Spoon the batter into the muffin molds.

Bake for 20–25 minutes until risen, firm and golden.

If using a pan, transfer the muffins to a wire rack; if using paper muffin cases, leave them in the cases and transfer them to the rack. Serve warm. Makes 9.

PER SERVING	
Calories	102
% Calories from fat	36
Fat (g)	4.5
Saturated fat (g)	0.8
Cholesterol (mg)	47.2
Sodium (mg)	250
Protein (g)	3.2
Carbohydrate (g)	14.4
Calcium (mg)	111.8

EXCHANGES	
Milk	0.0
Vegetable	0.0
Fruit	0.0
Bread	1.0
Meat	0.0
Fat	1.0

Just before shaping the rolls, knead in other ingredients such as sesame or sunflower seeds or currants for a different variation. Store in an airtight container for 2 days. Alternatively, the rolls will freeze well when fresh.

Polenta Bread Rolls

Serves 16 (1 roll per serving)

Polenta flour gives these rolls an interesting, slightly coarse texture and a golden color. Serve with hot soups or as sandwiches with various fillings. They are also good halved when cold, spread with crushed garlic and chopped herbs and then drizzled with olive oil. Wrap the rolls in aluminum foil and heat through in a hot oven for about 8 minutes for garlicky polenta rolls.

4–5 cups	bread flour (about 1 lb)	450 g
1 cup	fine polenta	220 g
1	1/4-oz packet active dry yeast	1
2 tsps	salt	2 tsps
1 3/4 cups	warm water	420 ml
2 tbsps	olive oil	30 ml

Grease a large baking sheet. In a large bowl, mix the flour, polenta and dry yeast together.

In a separate bowl, dissolve salt in warm water, then add the olive oil.

Pour this liquid into the flour, stirring well to form dough.

Tip the dough onto a floured work surface and knead for 5 minutes.

Shape into 16 equal-size balls and place them on the prepared baking sheet.

Sprinkle with a little extra polenta.

Leave to rise in warm place for about 40 minutes until doubled in size.

While the rolls are rising, pre-heat the oven to 425F.

Bake in the hot oven for about 15 minutes, but turn the oven down slightly halfway through the cooking.

The rolls should be risen and golden, and the underneath should sound hollow when tapped.

Transfer the rolls onto a rack to cool. Makes 16 rolls.

PER SERVING	
Calories	147
% Calories from fat	14
Fat (g)	2.3
Saturated fat (g)	0.3
Cholesterol (mg)	0
Sodium (mg)	292
Protein (g)	4.1
Carbohydrate (g)	27
Calcium (mg)	5.3

EXCHANGES	
Milk	0.0
Vegetable	0.0
Fruit	0.0
Bread	1.5
Meat	0.0
Fat	0.5

If you have a juicer, in this recipe you could use the leftover carrot pulp from making carrot juice.

Carrot and Raisin Cake with Lemon and Orange Frosting

Serves 9

This is a lovely nutritious cake, and the tangy frosting makes it a real treat. It would also be welcomed in packed lunch boxes or on picnics.

Cake

3/4 cup	sunflower oil	180 ml
3/4 cup	superfine sugar	170 g
3	large eggs, beaten	3
1/2 cup	raisins	1/2 cup
	grated zest from 1 lemon and 1 orange	
1–2	medium carrots, peeled and grated	1–2
3/4 cup	all-purpose flour	3/4 cup
2 tsps	ground cinnamon	2 tsps
	grating of nutmeg	
1 tsp	baking powder	1 tsp
1 tsp	baking soda	1 tsp

Frosting

1 tbsp	lemon juice	15 ml
1 tbsp	orange juice	15 ml
1 cup	(scant) confectioner's sugar, sifted	1 cup

Grease and line a 7-inch-square cake pan. Pre-heat the oven to 350F.

In a large bowl, beat the oil and sugar together. Gradually beat in the egg, raisins, zest and grated carrot.

Sift the flour, cinnamon, nutmeg and rising agents into the bowl and fold the cake mixture until well combined.

Tip the mixture into the cake pan, smoothing it out, and bake on the middle shelf of the oven for 35–40 minutes, until well risen and firm to the touch.

Allow to cool for about 10 minutes, then turn the cake out onto a rack and leave to cool completely.

To make the frosting: sift the sugar into a bowl and gradually beat in the lemon and orange juice until you have a smooth, glossy icing.

Place the cake on a serving plate and pour the icing over, allowing it to drizzle down the sides of the cake.

Once the icing has set, serve the cake cut into 9 squares.

PER SERVING	
Calories	373
% Calories from fat	47
Fat (g)	20
Saturated fat (g)	2.4
Cholesterol (mg)	70.8
Sodium (mg)	219
Protein (g)	3.6
Carbohydrate (g)	47.1
Calcium (mg)	59

EXCHANGES	
Milk	0.0
Vegetable	0.0
Fruit	0.0
Bread	3.0
Meat	0.0
Fat	3.5

Great for a messy children's treat, although make sure the filling has cooled properly.

Chocolate and Almond Pithiviers

Serves 6 (1 pithivier per serving)

This was inspired by a visit to the local pâtisserie while on vacation in France. It is a crisp pastry with a gooey chocolate and almond filling. Most French-style buns and cakes such as croissants, pain au chocolat and pain au raisin always contain butter, so it was a good reason to try these pithiviers.

½ cup	vegan margarine	110 g
½ cup	confectioner's sugar, sifted	½ cup
½ cup	chopped almonds	½ cup
1 tsp	vanilla extract	1 tsp
6 oz	dark, dairy-free chocolate, chopped	170 g
½ lb	puff pastry (dairy-free), shop bought	225 g
	egg for glazing	
1 tbsp	confectioner's sugar, sifted	1 tbsp
2 tbsps	sliced almonds, toasted	2 tbsps

Pre-heat the oven to 425F. In a medium bowl, beat the margarine with the sifted sugar until soft and smooth.

Stir in the almonds and vanilla and beat to a smooth paste, then tip in the chocolate and mix well.

On a floured surface, roll out the pastry to about ⅛ inch thick.

Cut out 12 rounds, using a small bowl about 4½ inches in diameter.

Spoon one-sixth of the chocolate paste into the center of 6 of the circles, leaving at least ½ inch around the edge; then brush the edges very lightly with water.

Place the 6 remaining circles over the tops to cover evenly.

Using a fork, press along edges, and refrigerate for about 30 minutes to allow to set.

Glaze with beaten egg. Bake for 12–15 minutes until risen and golden.

Remove from the oven, and allow to cool for about 5 minutes.

For icing, mix 1 tablespoon of sieved sugar with 1 tablespoon water until smooth.

Top the pithiviers with the icing, followed by a sprinkling of flaked almonds. Makes 6.

PER SERVING	
Calories	624
% Calories from fat	65
Fat (g)	46.9
Saturated fat (g)	13.1
Cholesterol (mg)	37.6
Sodium (mg)	284
Protein (g)	8
Carbohydrate (g)	48.7
Calcium (mg)	56.2

EXCHANGES	
Milk	0.0
Vegetable	0.0
Fruit	0.0
Bread	3.0
Meat	0.0
Fat	9.0

As the oat cakes cool they will become firm—if you can wait! They will store in a sealed container for 2–3 days.

Coconut and Chocolate Oat Cakes

Serves 12 (1 oat cake per serving)

The coconut and chocolate together make a delicious combination; the chocolate should remain as chunks when you bite into the oat cake. These cakes are gluten free as well as dairy free.

³/₄ cup	vegan margarine	170 g
³/₄ cup	dark corn syrup	180 g
1 cup	oats, uncooked	220 g
4 tbsps	dried coconut	4 tbsps
4 oz	dark, dairy-free chocolate, cut into small chunks	112 g

Pre-heat the oven to 350F. Grease a shallow, oblong baking pan measuring about 8 x 10 inches.

Melt the margarine with the syrup, stirring well, in a heavy pan over medium heat until dissolved. Remove from heat.

Stir in the oats and coconut, allow this to cool, then stir in chocolate chunks.

Pour into the baking pan and smooth down flat.

Bake for about 30 minutes until golden.

Allow to cool slightly for 5 minutes, then cut into squares. The cakes should become firm on cooling.

Turn out onto wire rack to cool completely. Makes about 12.

PER SERVING	
Calories	263
% Calories from fat	52
Fat (g)	15.9
Saturated fat (g)	4.7
Cholesterol (mg)	0.7
Sodium (mg)	165
Protein (g)	2.7
Carbohydrate (g)	30.5
Calcium (mg)	18.1

EXCHANGES	
Milk	0.0
Vegetable	0.0
Fruit	0.0
Bread	2.0
Meat	0.0
Fat	3.0

Make sure you don't give these to anyone with a nut allergy. Try using dark chocolate or pitted, chopped dates for different variations.

Raisin and Peanut Cookies

Serves 15 (1 cookie per serving)

These would be ideal to take on a picnic or put in a lunch box.

½ cup	soft vegan margarine	110 g
½ cup	brown or superfine sugar	110 g
1	egg, beaten	1
⅔ cup	self-rising flour	⅔ cup
1 tsp	pumpkin pie spice	1 tsp
½ cup	raisins	½ cup
½ cup	peanuts in skins, chopped	½ cup

Pre-heat the oven to 375F. Beat together all the ingredients, except the raisins and nuts, until well blended.

Mix in raisins and nuts, then, using a teaspoon, spoon onto greased baking sheets. Flatten them out into circles.

Bake for 10–15 minutes until golden brown around edges.

Cool slightly before lifting onto wire rack to cool completely. Makes about 15.

PER SERVING	
Calories	152
% Calories from fat	51
Fat (g)	8.9
Saturated fat (g)	1.7
Cholesterol (mg)	14.2
Sodium (mg)	150
Protein (g)	2.4
Carbohydrate (g)	16.8
Calcium (mg)	35

EXCHANGES	
Milk	0.0
Vegetable	0.0
Fruit	0.0
Bread	1.0
Meat	0.0
Fat	2.0

This should be eaten soon after rolling, as it will not store too well. Try making it with fresh raspberries.

Fresh Strawberry Cake Roll

Serves 6

The soy cream cheese is used as a substitute for heavy cream, and it combines wonderfully with the sweetened strawberries. This may be served as a cake or as a pudding.

Sponge Cake

3	eggs	3
3 tbsps	superfine sugar	75 g
1/2 tsp	vanilla extract	1/2 tsp
3 tbsps	all-purpose flour	3 tbsps
	pinch of salt	

Filling

3/4 cup	soy cream cheese	165 g
1 tbsp	soy cream	15 ml
1 tbsp	superfine sugar	25 g
1/2 tsp	vanilla extract	1/2 tsp
1 1/4 cups	fresh strawberries, hulled and sliced	1 1/4 cups

Cake: Pre-heat the oven to 350F. Grease a flat rectangular pan about 12 x 8 inches and 1 inch deep.

Cut a piece of waxed paper, allowing for an extra 2 inches on each side, and line it into the pan. Grease well with oil, and dust with flour and sugar.

Place eggs, sugar and vanilla in a double-boiler over simmering water. Whisk the mixture until light, thick and fluffy. Remove from the heat and continue whisking until cool.

Sift the flour and salt together, and, with a large metal spoon, gently fold it into the mixture, taking care not to beat out any of the air.

Carefully pour the mixture into the prepared pan, tipping it so the mixture fills all the corners. Bake in the middle of the oven for about 15 minutes.

The sponge is cooked if it has shrunk slightly and the edges look crinkled. When pressed gently it will feel firm but spongy.

Lift the waxed paper with the sponge in it and cover with a clean, slightly damp tea towel and leave to cool.

Filling: In a small bowl, mix the cream cheese with the soy cream, beating well until smooth. Add sugar to taste and the vanilla extract.

Spread this cream mixture over the cake and top with sliced strawberries, reserving about 20 slices to decorate.

PER SERVING	
Calories	176
% Calories from fat	55
Fat (g)	10.8
Saturated fat (g)	2.8
Cholesterol (mg)	106.2
Sodium (mg)	167.9
Protein (g)	4.7
Carbohydrate (g)	14.6
Calcium (mg)	17.2

EXCHANGES	
Milk	0.0
Vegetable	0.0
Fruit	0.0
Bread	1.0
Meat	0.0
Fat	2.0

Keeping longest edge nearest you, hold each front edge of the waxed paper and slowly roll up the cake, pulling away the waxed paper as you roll.

Alternatively, cut the cake into 2 equal squares, spread filling over one, and top it off with the other square.

Place on a serving plate and decorate with sieved confectioner's sugar and remaining strawberries.

Refrigerate before serving.

Wash the orange well, and if possible use an organic one.

Orange and Almond Shortbread

Serves 16 (1 shortbread per serving)

The orange zest gives these breads a delicious flavor. They would also be equally good using lemon zest and chopped hazelnuts.

3/4 cup	vegan margarine	170 g
3 tbsps	superfine sugar	75 g
1	large orange, zest only	1
	few drops of almond extract	
2 tbsps	ground almonds	2 tbsps
2 tbsps	ground rice	50 g
3/4 cup	all-purpose flour	3/4 cup

Pre-heat the oven to 375F. Beat the margarine with the sugar until soft and creamy.

Using a vegetable peeler, peel rind carefully off the orange, trying just to get outer zest and not the pith. Then cut the zest into little pieces.

Mix the orange peelings with the sugar mixture, adding the almond extract and finally the almonds, ground rice and flour.

Work it together to form a ball, leaving the bowl clean.

Lay the dough on a large, greased baking sheet and press into an 8 x 8-inch square about 1/2 inch thick.

Prick the shortbread all over with a fork and mark out into finger shapes; sprinkle with extra sugar.

Bake for about 20 minutes until a pale golden color.

Allow to cool and become firm before cutting and transferring to a serving plate. Makes 12–16.

PER SERVING	
Calories	119
% Calories from fat	68
Fat (g)	9.1
Saturated fat (g)	1.7
Cholesterol (mg)	0
Sodium (mg)	100
Protein (g)	1
Carbohydrate (g)	8.5
Calcium (mg)	9.4

EXCHANGES	
Milk	0.0
Vegetable	0.0
Fruit	0.0
Bread	0.5
Meat	0.0
Fat	2.0

If you don't like walnuts, hazelnuts or pecans are a suitable alternative. Use half whole wheat flour if preferred.

Spiced Apple and Walnut Cake

Serves 8

This cake is one of my favorites. Serve for snacks or as a hot pudding with soy yogurt. Or how about trying it with the Oat and Honey Cream recipe on page 169?

1/2 cup	vegan margarine	110 g
3/4 cup	brown sugar	165 g
2	eggs, beaten	2
1 cup	all-purpose flour	1 cup
1 tsp	pumpkin pie spice	1 tsp
1 tsp	ground cinnamon	1 tsp
	grated nutmeg	
2 tsps	baking powder	2 tsps
1 cup	peeled and finely chopped cooking apple	220 g
3 tbsps	walnuts, chopped	3 tbsps
3 tbsps	soy milk	45 ml

Pre-heat the oven to 350F. Grease and line a deep 7-inch-diameter round cake pan with waxed paper.

In a large bowl, cream the margarine and sugar until pale and fluffy.

Add the eggs a little at a time, beating well.

Sift the flour, spices and baking powder into the bowl and stir into the mixture.

Fold in the chopped apples, walnuts and soy milk to make soft, dropping consistency.

Pour the mixture into the prepared pan and bake for about 1 hour. Check after about 40 minutes, and if necessary turn down heat. When cooked, the cake should be well risen and firm to touch.

Turn out onto a rack to cool. Makes 8–10 slices.

PER SERVING	
Calories	285
% Calories from fat	46
Fat (g)	14.8
Saturated fat (g)	2.8
Cholesterol (mg)	53.1
Sodium (mg)	280
Protein (g)	3.9
Carbohydrate (g)	35.5
Calcium (mg)	106.7

EXCHANGES	
Milk	0.0
Vegetable	0.0
Fruit	0.0
Bread	2.0
Meat	0.0
Fat	3.0

For a lemon or orange layer cake, use this same sponge recipe without cocoa but with orange or lemon zest. Then fill with lemon butter icing (made with vegan margarine), and top with lemon icing.

Wicked Chocolate Cake

Serves 8

A fabulous birthday party cake that will not leave the children feeling they have missed out.

Decorate with shavings of dark chocolate, using a vegetable peeler.

Sponge Cake

1/2 cup	soft vegan margarine	110 g
1/2 cup	superfine sugar	110 g
2	eggs, beaten	2
1/2 cup	self-rising flour, sifted	1/2 cup
1 tbsp	cocoa (omit cocoa for a plain sponge)	1 tbsp

Icing

2 tbsps	vegan margarine	50 g
3 oz	dark, dairy-free chocolate, broken up	85 g
3/4 cup	confectioner's sugar	3/4 cup

Cake: Pre-heat the oven to 325F. Line the base of two 7-inch sponge cake pans with waxed paper and lightly oil.

Cream together the margarine and sugar until light and fluffy, then gradually beat in the eggs.

Fold in the sifted flour and cocoa.

Pour evenly into the prepared pans, and smooth the mixture down.

Bake for 25–30 minutes.

Remove from the oven, loosen the edges and turn out onto a rack to cool.

Meanwhile, make the icing.

Icing: Put the margarine and chocolate into a double-boiler over hot water until the chocolate and margarine melt; mix well.

Beat in the sifted sugar and allow the icing to cool slightly.

To assemble: Lay one sponge on a plate, spoon over one-third of the icing and smear over evenly.

Cover with the other half of cake and spoon over the remaining icing.

Using a knife, smooth icing evenly around the sides of the cake.

PER SERVING	
Calories	319
% Calories from fat	52
Fat (g)	19.2
Saturated fat (g)	5.3
Cholesterol (mg)	53.9
Sodium (mg)	282
Protein (g)	3
Carbohydrate (g)	36.2
Calcium (mg)	41.5

EXCHANGES	
Milk	0.0
Vegetable	0.0
Fruit	0.0
Bread	2.0
Meat	0.0
Fat	4.0

Cornmeal Pastry

The result is a crisp pastry that makes a pleasant change from ordinary pastry. I use this pastry to make the Mexican-style Avocado and Shrimp Empañadas (see page 22). Try all sorts of fillings with this pastry for a picnic or crisp snack.

1 cup	(scant) plain white flour	1 cup
²/₃ cup	cornmeal	²/₃ cup
1 tsp	salt	1 tsp
6 tbsps	olive or vegetable oil	90 ml
1	egg, beaten	1
	dash of cold water	

Combine the flour, cornmeal and salt in a bowl.

Stir in the oil and beaten egg and enough water to make ingredients cling together.

Knead dough on lightly floured surface until it forms a smooth ball.

Cover and chill until required. Makes about 14 oz, enough for one 8-inch pie crust.

PER RECIPE

Calories	1582
% Calories from fat	51
Fat (g)	88.7
Saturated fat (g)	12.9
Cholesterol (mg)	212.5
Sodium (mg)	2394
Protein (g)	27
Carbohydrate (g)	167.5
Calcium (mg)	49.3

EXCHANGES

Milk	0.0
Vegetable	0.0
Fruit	0.0
Bread	11.0
Meat	0.0
Fat	17.0

Crisp Sweet Pastry

Sweet pastry generally cannot be bought commercially without containing dairy products. This variation is a lovely crisp, biscuity pastry, which will match up to any others of its kind, making it ideal for fresh fruit pies.

3/4 cup	all-purpose flour	3/4 cup
	pinch of salt	
3 tbsps	vegan margarine	75 g
3	medium egg yolks	3
3 tbsps	superfine sugar	75 g
	few drops vanilla extract	

Sift the flour and salt into a large bowl.

Cut the margarine into small chunks and, using the tips of your fingers, rub the margarine into the flour until the mixture resembles breadcrumbs.

Make a well in the center of the flour and add the yolks, sugar and vanilla. Using a knife, work in all the surrounding flour, then gently knead until smooth.

Place in bag and chill for at least 30 minutes.

Use as instructed. Makes about 1 1/8 cups (14 oz), enough for one 8-inch pie crust.

PER RECIPE	
Calories	963
% Calories from fat	47
Fat (g)	50.3
Saturated fat (g)	11.6
Cholesterol (mg)	637.9
Sodium (mg)	423
Protein (g)	18.4
Carbohydrate (g)	108.8
Calcium (mg)	95.3

EXCHANGES	
Milk	0.0
Vegetable	0.0
Fruit	0.0
Bread	7.0
Meat	0.0
Fat	10.0

Quick Flaky Pastry

This is a fairly easy crispy light pastry that can be used as a substitute for puff pastry if you are unable to buy it.

³/₄ cup	vegan margarine	165 g
1 cup	all-purpose flour	1 cup
¹/₂ tsp	salt	¹/₂ tsp
	cold water to mix	

Put the margarine in the freezer for about 1 hour.
Sift the flour and salt into a bowl.
Dip the margarine in the flour and quickly grate into the bowl.
Using a knife, mix the margarine into the flour. Gradually add some cold water a little at a time and, using a knife, mix to form dough that leaves the bowl clean.
Quickly bring together to form a ball with your hands.
Chill in the fridge for half an hour.
Use as required. Makes about 12 oz, enough for one 9-inch pie crust.

PER RECIPE	
Calories	1671
% Calories from fat	73
Fat (g)	137.4
Saturated fat (g)	26.9
Cholesterol (mg)	0
Sodium (mg)	2761
Protein (g)	14.4
Carbohydrate (g)	96.9
Calcium (mg)	70.2
EXCHANGES	
Milk	0.0
Vegetable	0.0
Fruit	0.0
Bread	7.0
Meat	0.0
Fat	27.0

Shortcrust Pastry

2 tbsps	vegan margarine	50 g
2 tbsps	lard	50 g
1 cup	all-purpose flour, sifted	1 cup
2 tbsps	cold water	30 ml
	pinch salt	

Rub the fats into the sifted flour and salt until the mixture resembles breadcrumbs.
Using a knife, add the water and mix to form a firm dough.
Cover and refrigerate for at least 30 minutes before using.
Makes about 1¹/₂ cups (12 oz), enough for one 9-inch pie crust.

PER RECIPE	
Calories	885
% Calories from fat	50
Fat (g)	49.1
Saturated fat (g)	14.5
Cholesterol (mg)	23.9
Sodium (mg)	268
Protein (g)	13.2
Carbohydrate (g)	95.6
Calcium (mg)	27.2
EXCHANGES	
Milk	0.0
Vegetable	0.0
Fruit	0.0
Bread	6.0
Meat	0.0
Fat	10.0

Take care not to overcook as it will burn easily, giving the pastry a bitter taste.

Whole Wheat Pastry

For a more wholesome pastry, use this recipe. This pastry rolls out quite thinly and does not require as much pre-cooking as shortcrust. The baking powder gives it a lighter texture.

The pastry should be left to rest longer than ordinary shortcrust for the flour to absorb the liquid.

1 cup	whole wheat flour	1 cup
2 tsps	baking powder	2 tsps
	pinch of salt	
2 tbsps	vegan margarine	50 g
2 tbsps	vegetable shortening	50 g
1 tsp	brown sugar	8 g
2 tbsps	vegetable oil	30 ml
6 tbsps	cold water	90 ml

In a large bowl, mix the flour, salt and baking powder. Lightly rub in the fats until the mixture resembles breadcrumbs.

Combine sugar, oil and water and pour into flour.

Using knife blade, mix to light dough consistency.

Cover and refrigerate for at least 1 hour before using.

Makes about 12 oz, enough for one 9-inch pie crust.

PER RECIPE	
Calories	1092
% Calories from fat	61
Fat (g)	76.1
Saturated fat (g)	14.3
Cholesterol (mg)	0
Sodium (mg)	1249
Protein (g)	16.7
Carbohydrate (g)	94.3
Calcium (mg)	613.7

EXCHANGES	
Milk	0.0
Vegetable	0.0
Fruit	0.0
Bread	6.0
Meat	0.0
Fat	15.0

Try chocolate muffins for a special treat by substituting dark chocolate chunks.

Blueberry Muffins

Serves 8 (1 muffin per serving)

These are very quick and simple to make and a favorite with my children for breakfast or lunch; I think it is because blueberries are not as sharp as some fruit such as black currants. However, you could use other fruits or even dried fruits instead of the blueberries.

1¼ cups	self-rising flour	1¼ cups
⅔ cup	brown sugar	150 g
1	egg, beaten	1
1 cup	(scant) soy milk	200 ml
3½ tbsps	sunflower oil	53 ml
⅔ cup	blueberries, rinsed	⅔ cup

Pre-heat the oven to 350F. Use either large paper muffin shells or a pan with 1-cup-capacity holes, well greased.

Sift the flour with the sugar, add the egg, soy milk and oil and beat well.

Stir in the blueberries.

Spoon mixture into prepared pan or the paper shells.

Bake in the oven for 20–25 minutes until risen and golden.

Place on a wire rack, and serve warm. Makes about 8 big muffins.

PER SERVING	
Calories	217
% Calories from fat	30
Fat (g)	7.4
Saturated fat (g)	0.9
Cholesterol (mg)	26.6
Sodium (mg)	267
Protein (g)	3.6
Carbohydrate (g)	34.7
Calcium (mg)	86.6

EXCHANGES	
Milk	0.0
Vegetable	0.0
Fruit	0.0
Bread	2.0
Meat	0.0
Fat	1.5

Corn Griddle Cakes

Serves 4 (2 cakes per serving)

These are delicious served with crisp bacon and maple syrup for a lactose-free breakfast.

1/2 cup	all-purpose flour	1/2 cup
1 tsp	baking powder	1 tsp
1/2 tsp	paprika	1/2 tsp
1/2 tsp	salt	1/2 tsp
1	egg, beaten	1
2/3 cup	soy milk	150 ml
1/2 cup	sweetcorn—either fresh off cob and quickly boiled, frozen or canned and drained	110 g
1 tbsp	sunflower oil	15 ml
	extra oil for frying	

Sift the dry ingredients into a bowl. Beat in the egg and then gradually add the soy milk until you have a smooth batter.

Stir in the sweetcorn and a tablespoon of oil.

Heat a large griddle pan or heavy frying pan, and pour on about 1 teaspoon oil.

Spoon out about 1 large heaping tablespoon of batter for each griddle cake.

Cook until the bubbles show on the surface, then turn the cakes over and cook the other sides until golden brown (about 1 minute on either side).

Serve on warmed plates. Makes about 8 cakes.

PER SERVING	
Calories	137
% Calories from fat	37
Fat (g)	5.7
Saturated fat (g)	0.9
Cholesterol (mg)	53.1
Sodium (mg)	435
Protein (g)	4.9
Carbohydrate (g)	17.3
Calcium (mg)	79.1

EXCHANGES	
Milk	0.0
Vegetable	0.0
Fruit	0.0
Bread	1.0
Meat	0.0
Fat	1.0

Most smoked white fish such as trout would be suitable for this dish. Garam masala is an Indian spice that can be found in ethnic aisles and Indian grocery stores.

Kedgeree

Serves 4

Kedgeree makes a hearty breakfast, one that even the children should enjoy. We often have it as a light supper, and any leftover I heat up for a quick breakfast.

Alternatively, serve hot for lunch or a light supper with the Creamy Curried Coconut Sauce (see page 116). It would also be an impressive starter for 8 if reheated in ramekins and turned onto small plates with the sauce poured around the edge.

1 lb	smoked haddock fillet, or cooked fresh salmon if preferred	450 g
1 cup	basmati rice	1 cup
1	medium onion, finely chopped	1
1 tbsp	vegan margarine	25 g
1 tsp	garam masala	1 tsp
1 tsp	ground cumin	1 tsp
1/2 tsp	ground turmeric	1/2 tsp
4	hard-boiled eggs, cut into quarters	4
2 tbsps	freshly chopped parsley	2 tbsps
	juice of half a lemon	
	salt and freshly ground pepper	

Pre-heat the oven to 375F. Bring a pan half-filled with water to a boil, and simmer the haddock for about 10 minutes—do not overcook.

Drain the fish, saving the cooking water. Remove the skin and bones and flake the fish.

Add a little more water and cook the rice in the fish water until just tender. Drain and allow to dry out a little.

Gently sauté the onion in the margarine for about 8 minutes until softened, add the spices and cook for a further 3 minutes. Remove from heat.

In a large, warm baking dish, combine the rice with the spiced onion mixture, eggs, parsley, lemon juice and flaked fish. Season with freshly ground pepper and salt only if haddock is not too salty.

Cover with aluminum foil and heat through in the oven for 15–20 minutes until piping hot.

PER SERVING	
Calories	399
% Calories from fat	23
Fat (g)	10.2
Saturated fat (g)	2.3
Cholesterol (mg)	299.8
Sodium (mg)	965
Protein (g)	38.5
Carbohydrate (g)	37
Calcium (mg)	117.9
EXCHANGES	
Milk	0.0
Vegetable	0.0
Fruit	0.0
Bread	2.5
Meat	4.0
Fat	0.0

For a light supper, try adding chopped ham to the eggs before frying.

French Toast

Serves 4

This is especially enjoyed in our house for breakfast or a quick lunch. Complement it with crispy bacon and maple syrup.

3	eggs, beaten	3
1 tbsp	soy milk	15 ml
	pinch of salt	
4	thick slices of white or brown bread	4
2 tbsps	sunflower oil for frying	30 ml

Heat a large frying pan with half the oil over medium heat. Mix the eggs with milk and salt.

Dip the bread slices in the egg, allowing them to soak up as much as possible.

Turn the bread over and soak the other side.

Lift bread out of egg mixture, allowing excess to fall back into bowl.

Place in a hot frying pan, cook for 1–2 minutes, turn and repeat.

The French toast should be golden and cooked through. Serve immediately.

PER SERVING	
Calories	237
% Calories from fat	49
Fat (g)	13.6
Saturated fat (g)	1.9
Cholesterol (mg)	209.4
Sodium (mg)	288
Protein (g)	10.8
Carbohydrate (g)	20.5
Calcium (mg)	58.5
EXCHANGES	
Milk	0.0
Vegetable	0.0
Fruit	0.0
Bread	1.5
Meat	0.0
Fat	3.0

For an iced shake, try chopping up the banana and freezing it before blending. Try experimenting with other fruits such as strawberries, peaches, raspberries, etc.

Banana Oat Shake

Serves 2

This is a creamy alternative to a milkshake and a lot better for you! The shake would be good for babies or toddlers (omitting honey for very young babies).

2	large ripe bananas	2
1½ cups	chilled Oat and Honey Cream (see page 169)	360 ml

Blend the two ingredients together in a blender or processor. Pour into two glasses and serve immediately.

PER SERVING	
Calories	200
% Calories from fat	5
Fat (g)	1.1
Saturated fat (g)	0.3
Cholesterol (mg)	0
Sodium (mg)	2
Protein (g)	2.3
Carbohydrate (g)	50.1
Calcium (mg)	11.9
EXCHANGES	
Milk	0.0
Vegetable	0.0
Fruit	1.0
Bread	2.0
Meat	0.0
Fat	0.0

Supermarkets stock frozen summer fruits that can be used all year round.

Summer Berry Fruit Crush

Serves 2

This is pleasantly cooling and refreshing on hot summer days. Experiment with all different fruits, depending on the season. Peaches, melons or any other soft fruit would also create a delicious fruit crush.

¹/₂ cup	strawberries	¹/₂ cup
¹/₂ cup	raspberries	¹/₂ cup
1 cup	apple juice	240 ml
4	ice cubes	4
	clear honey or sugar to taste	

Using a blender, mix all the ingredients, excluding the ice. Sieve the mixture to remove any seeds. Return to blender with the ice cubes to finish the crush.

Serve immediately.

PER SERVING	
Calories	84
% Calories from fat	4
Fat (g)	0.4
Saturated fat (g)	0
Cholesterol (mg)	0
Sodium (mg)	4
Protein (g)	0.6
Carbohydrate (g)	20.6
Calcium (mg)	20.5
EXCHANGES	
Milk	0.0
Vegetable	0.0
Fruit	1.5
Bread	0.0
Meat	0.0
Fat	0.0

Helpful Organizations

American Academy of Allergy, Asthma & Immunology
611 East Wells Street
Milwaukee, WI 53202
Phone: (414) 272-6071
Fax: (414) 272-6070
Email: info@aaaai.org
Internet: www.aaaai.org

American Dairy Goat Association
209 West Main Street
Spindale, NC 28160
Phone: (828) 286-3801
Fax: (828) 287-0476
Email: info@adga.org
Internet: www.adga.org

American Dietetic Association (ADA)
216 West Jackson Boulevard
Chicago, IL 60606-6995
Phone: (312) 899-0040
Fax: (312) 899-1979
Internet: www.eatright.org

American Gastroenterological Association
7910 Woodmont Avenue, Seventh Floor
Bethesda, MD 20814
Phone: (301) 654-2055
Fax: (301) 652-3890
Email: webinfo@gastro.org
Internet: www.gastro.org

Anaphylaxis Canada
416 Moore Avenue, Suite 306
Toronto, ON M4G 1C9
Phone: (416) 785-5666
Fax: (416) 785-0458
Email: info@anaphylaxis.ca
Internet: www.anaphylaxis.org

The College of Family Physicians of Canada
2630 Skymark Avenue
Mississauga, ON L4W 5A4
Phone: (905) 629-0900
Toll Free: (800) 387-6197
Fax: (905) 629-0893
Internet: www.cfpc.ca

Dietitians of Canada
480 University Avenue, Suite 604
Toronto, ON M5G 1V2
Phone: (416) 596-0857
Fax: (416) 596-0603
Internet: www.dietitians.ca

The Food Allergy & Anaphylaxis Network
10400 Eaton Place, Suite 107
Fairfax, VA 22030-2208
Phone: (800) 929-4040
Fax: (703) 691-2713
Email: faan@foodallergy.org
Internet: www.foodallergy.org

Foundation for Digestive Health and Nutrition
7910 Woodmont Avenue, Suite 610
Bethesda, MD 20814-3015
Phone: (301) 222-4002
Fax: (301) 222-4010
Email: info@fdhn.org
Internet: www.fdhn.org

International Food Information Council Foundation
1100 Connecticut Avenue N.W., Suite 430
Washington, DC 20036
Phone: (202) 296-6540
Fax: (202) 296-6547
Email: foodinfo@ific.org
Internet: www.ific.org

International Foundation for Functional Gastrointestinal Disorders (IFFGD)
P.O. Box 170864
Milwaukee, WI 53217
Phone: (888) 964-2001 or (414) 964-1799
Fax: (414) 964-7176
Email: iffgd@iffgd.org
Internet: www.iffgd.org

National Digestive Diseases Information Clearinghouse
2 Information Way
Bethesda, MD 20892-3570
Phone: (800) 891-5389
Fax: (301) 907-8906
Email: nddic@info.niddk.nih.gov
Internet: www.niddk.nih.gov

National Institute of Nutrition
302-265 Carling Avenue
Ottawa, ON K1S 2E1
Phone: (613) 235-3355
Fax: (613) 235-7032
Email: nin@nin.ca
Internet: www.nin.ca

Index